D1470221

The plethora of books and articles about leadership can be mind-numbing. But there is always room for a book that centers on Jesus, the leader servant. I think the essence of this message is a fresh glimpse of Jesus, the one whose exercise of leadership is so radically different from the success-satiated tripe that gets promoted in our contemporary understanding of the concept. My hope is that this volume will draw us to a fresh encounter with Jesus and, through that, a transformation in how we lead as genuine servants.

SAM METCALF
President, CRM (Christian Resource Ministries)

Compassionate leadership—what leader doesn't want that?! This book is authentic because it was written by two compassionate leaders. My friends Dr. Ted Engstrom and Dr. Paul Cedar show that compassionate leadership is biblical leadership—it's Christ-like leadership.

DR. RAYMOND ORTLUND
President, Renewal Ministries
Former Speaker, *Haven of Rest* Radio Broadcast

In an era of brash leaders, corporate raiders and harsh "take no prisoners" corporate models of leadership, *Compassionate Leadership* is an oasis of truth and reason that offers a radically different approach. Christian leaders should look first to these biblical principles of leadership before looking to the Fortune 500 for their role models.

RICH STEARNS
President, World Vision U. S.

After reading so many so-called "Christian" books based on business models of leadership, it's good to read one that is based on the biblical model of the caring shepherd and the biblical motivation of love. I highly recommend this book to beginners and veterans alike.

WARREN W. WIERSBE
Author and Bible Teacher

TED ENGSTROM
& PAUL CEDAR

COMPASSIONATE
LEADERSHIP

Regal

From Gospel Light
Ventura, California, U.S.A.

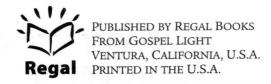

PUBLISHED BY REGAL BOOKS
FROM GOSPEL LIGHT
VENTURA, CALIFORNIA, U.S.A.
PRINTED IN THE U.S.A.

Regal Books is a ministry of Gospel Light, a Christian publisher dedicated to serving the local church. We believe God's vision for Gospel Light is to provide church leaders with biblical, user-friendly materials that will help them evangelize, disciple and minister to children, youth and families.

It is our prayer that this Regal book will help you discover biblical truth for your own life and help you meet the needs of others. May God richly bless you.

For a free catalog of resources from Regal Books/Gospel Light, please call your Christian supplier or contact us at 1-800-4-GOSPEL *or* www.regalbooks.com.

Library of Congress Cataloging-in-Publication Data
Engstrom, Theodore Wilhelm, 1916-
   Compassionate leadership / Ted W. Engstrom, Paul A. Cedar.
      p. cm.
   ISBN 0-8307-4188-7 (hard cover)
   1. Leadership—Religious aspects—Christianity. 2. Service (Theology). 3. Compassion—Religious aspects—Christianity. I. Cedar, Paul A., 1938- II. Title.
   BV4597.53.L43E54 2006
   253—dc22   2006006851

1   2   3   4   5   6   7   8   9   10   /   12   11   10   09   08   07   06

Rights for publishing this book in other languages are contracted by Gospel Light Worldwide, the international nonprofit ministry of Gospel Light. Gospel Light Worldwide also provides publishing and technical assistance to international publishers dedicated to producing Sunday School and Vacation Bible School curricula and books in the languages of the world. For additional information, visit www.gospellightworldwide.org; write to Gospel Light Worldwide, P.O. Box 3875, Ventura, CA 93006; or send an e-mail to info@gospellightworldwide.org.

CONTENTS

ACKNOWLEDGMENTS

As co-authors of this book, we are indebted to a fellow gifted author, Norman Rohrer, for his editorial assistance in bringing together our thoughts and gleaning from earlier writings for this publication. Norm himself is a gifted author, and he has given dedicated service to us, his friends, in this project. For this we are most grateful.

FOREWORD
Dan Kimball

Reading this book is very much like listening to one of Johnny Cash's more recent CDs. When you hear the voice and music of Johnny Cash, you can instinctively tell that he is a seasoned, vintage musician. Johnny Cash has become a guru—you could say even a mentor—to emerging generations looking for someone who sings from the depth and breadth of a lifelong experience. What was interesting about Johnny Cash is that toward the end of his life, more than ever he was openly and strongly pointing to Jesus and the wisdom of the Bible. His last album, "My Mother's Hymn Book," was comprised entirely of hymns dedicated to his faith in Jesus.

This book is similar in that it draws on the breadth and depth of the lifelong experience and leadership wisdom of Ted Engstrom and Paul Cedar. Here we have the rare opportunity to study under two men whom I consider to be the leadership gurus and older mentors today's emerging generation is looking for. After a lifetime of studying, writing about and practicing leadership, Ted and Paul openly and strongly point to the wisdom of the Bible and the example of Jesus, who was truly the model of being a servant and leading by compassion.

As leadership trends come and go, books are written on everything from crafting mission statements to setting strategic goals to being able to develop multiple levels of ministry teams. These are all much needed in ministry—it is a fast-paced and complex world that we live in. But what makes this book stand out from the rest is that it is written by two men who are not just popping in on the leadership scene with new and trendy ideas that may sound good.

Ted and Paul have observed leadership trends over a long period of time, and this book is filled with wisdom that we should all prayerfully absorb. The plethora of leadership principles and strategies out there today may fade away as culture shifts and leadership values change. But like a Johnny Cash song, the words in this book penetrate beyond any trend or fad. They emerge from a pool of deep wisdom. They speak from and to the heart of what leadership is about and will outlast any trend or fad—leading like Jesus with a heart and life of compassion and servanthood.

Dan Kimball
Author, *The Emerging Church*
www.vintagefaith.com

FOREWORD
Leighton Ford

An old Indian proverb says that "nothing grows under the banyan tree." That huge tree towers so high and spreads its branches so wide with such thick foliage that the sun cannot filter through to nurture the tiny seedlings below.

The same thing, unfortunately, can be said of many visible and strong human leaders. Their reach goes high. Their influence goes wide. They are seen by many as leaders. And yet they do not create space within their circle of influence to permit younger leaders to put down their roots and spread their branches.

That was not Jesus' kind of leadership. As tall as He stood, being the Son of God among men, He still humbled Himself and took the place of a servant—even submitting to death on the cross for our sake.

And His goal was to reproduce other compassionate leaders who would lead by serving. "The Son of man came not to be served but to serve," He once reminded His quarreling disciples (see Mark 10:45). And again, when He had washed and dried their feet at His last supper with them, He said, "Now that I, your Lord and Teacher, have washed your feet, you also should wash one another's feet. I have set you an example that you should do as I have done for you" (John 13:14-15).

It is this "Jesus style" of leadership that our world needs today, when the media hypes leaders as being super-personalities, who too often have super-sized egos, while followers hunger for those with the authentic spirit of compassionate service shown by Jesus.

Paul Cedar and Ted Engstrom have given us their thoughts on compassionate, service-oriented leadership with an authenticity that is evident both in their source and in their example.

Their source book, of course, is the Bible, particularly the Gospel stories of Jesus. Many "Christian" leadership books preach the false gospel of secular leadership models, hiding their true message behind some carefully selected Bible verses. Ted and Paul, however, have gone to the Source—drawing on the life and ministry of Jesus Himself.

Then, too, the convictions they express have been forged in their own lives. Across the years both have been followers, and both have been leaders.

Ted Engstrom led in Youth for Christ, in religious publishing, and then was second in command to the legendary Bob Pierce in World Vision. After assisting two presidents of this dynamic organization, he himself became a most effective president.

Similarly, Paul Cedar was part of the Billy Graham team; then he worked closely with me as the director of several of my own evangelistic campaigns. Later as a pastor of two outstanding churches, as president of the Evangelical Free Church of America, and then while heading the Mission America Coalition and chairing the Lausanne Committee for World Evangelization, he consistently exhibited a sense of compassionate leadership as he served the people of God.

What do these two men have in common? First, they always sought to be led by Jesus and to exalt God, not their own egos. Second, they have been Kingdom seekers, not empire builders, aiming not at building their own reputations but at working in close partnership with others. Third, both of them have been mentors to younger leaders, seeking to pour out their lives into the next generation and to make room for that next generation to grow. More than one outstanding leader has told me of the formative influence either Paul or Ted or both have had in their lives.

They are not "banyan tree" leaders. Rather, they have sought to lead others to Jesus, like Jesus, for Jesus. . . and always to be led by Him.

Out of their leadership experience Paul and Ted have distilled some crucial truths which they have lived out—and which they desire to share with you.

This is a simple, direct, accessible book. It reminds me of a saying of the late Bertrand Russell who said that he would give nothing for a simplicity that comes before complexity, but would give anything for the simplicity that comes after complexity.

Through many years, in varied situations and during complex leadership challenges, the authors have come to the simplicity that is in (or, toward) Jesus.

I hope many current and emerging leaders will find that same spirit of compassionate leadership and live it out through simple acts of service.

Leighton Ford, President
Leighton Ford Ministries
Charlotte, North Carolina

INTRODUCTION

Discussions about leadership usually focus on power, management or organization. In recent years Christians have often added the word "servant" to their leadership discussions. Today, we go one step further and add the word "compassionate." These two adjectives—the broader "servant" and the more focused "compassionate"—thrust leadership discussions into a new and blessed dimension.

Like any spiritual discipline, compassionate servant leadership is neither easy nor natural. But anyone can reach the goal by submitting to Christ as Lord and applying some basic principles of His Word to their daily lives.

This book will cover both the broader ideal of being a servant and the specific expression of compassion. Our thesis is found in the words of our Lord who said, "Whoever wishes to become great among you shall be your servant. . . . For the son of Man did not come to be served, but to serve" (Mark 10:34). This explodes the myth that leaders are more important than followers.

All mature Christians are leaders who serve. All leaders who truly serve will show compassion. They know how to "build themselves up in [their] most holy faith" (Jude 20). And they constantly encourage and enable other believers as well to grow in the grace and knowledge of Jesus Christ. In a word, they seek to develop disciples of Jesus, not of themselves. And they attempt to go about it in the same manner Jesus went about it.

"Drive hard with a light hand" is an equestrian principle that can lead to success in other areas of life, including the discipline of servant leadership. Our Lord promised that although servant leaders may work harder, they also experience an abundance of deep-down joy.

Jesus' call to be compassionate leaders who serve underscores the paradox of the Christian's life: "Whoever wants to be great among you must be your servant, and whoever wants to be first must be your slave—just as the Son of Man did not come to be served, but to serve, and to give his life as a ransom for many" (Matt. 20:26-28).

Do you want to be a compassionate leader who serves? Then start with these simple guidelines.

Be Generous

After the Day of Pentecost, when an intense rabbi named Saul took the Damascus Road and ran straight into the arms of Jesus, the apostles were suspicious. "This murderer is faking it!" they said when Saul's conversion reached their ears. "It's his subversive trick to get inside the Church."

Barnabas (the Son of Encouragement) met him when Saul arrived in Jerusalem from Damascus. "Saul has seen the Lord," he later told his brethren. "In Damascus he preached the gospel fearlessly. This man Paul is for real."

Believe and Help

As the two believers prepared to launch out as missionaries, Barnabas suggested to Paul that they take John Mark with them. But Paul was adamantly opposed. Barnabas was willing to risk his relationship with the apostle by standing firm for John Mark. "Sorry, Paul," he said. "I'm not going to let you do that to this young man. You'll wipe him out."

Encourage Everyone

The question of association with Grecian Jews surfaced in Jerusalem. Paul was away; Peter was still in process and couldn't handle the assignment; Judaizers in the church were unprepared for the debates.

Barnabas had no prejudice. The "Son of Encouragement" happily volunteered. And when he got to Jerusalem, he was *thrilled* by reports of God at work in their midst.

Get Excited

Before Pentecost, when the apostles cast lots to fill the vacancy left by the death of Judas, the lot fell upon Matthias. The one who lost was Joseph called Barnabas. Joseph was called, but not elected to become the twelfth apostle. Did he pout? Did he feel hurt, retreat and lick his wounds? Not for a moment. Joseph the Levite—Barnabas himself—is the one who lost so it's easy to see why he fought so hard for the underdog. Why did Barnabas sell his property and give it to the struggling Church? Why did he step in when every other believer was suspicious of Saul? Why did he risk the success of a missionary trip with the unpopular John Mark? Why did he try to unite the squabbling Jews and Christians in Jerusalem? He did so because he knew what it was like being on the outside looking in.

Help Others

Joseph's name was changed to "Son of Encouragement" to match his character. If someone changed your name to correspond to your lifestyle, what would they call you? Would they call you "Son of Compassion"? How about "The Leader Who Serves"?

Here is my servant, whom I uphold, my chosen one in whom I delight; I will put my Spirit on him and he will bring justice to the nations. He will not shout or cry out, or raise his voice in the streets. A bruised reed he will not break, and a smoldering wick he will not snuff out. In faithfulness, he will bring forth justice; he will not falter or be discouraged till he establishes justice on earth. In his law the islands will put their hope (Isa. 42:1-4).

The scriptural admonitions in this book have been tested by the authors in the crucible of combined experiences. May this book inspire you to obey the first compassionate leader who served—the One who has reminded us: "Inasmuch as you did it to one of the least of these My brethren, you did it to Me" (Matt. 25:40, *NKJV*).

CHAPTER ONE

PORTRAIT OF A COMPASSIONATE LEADER

I n the upper room of a building in Jerusalem, just before the Passover Feast, our Lord offered a perfect example of a leader who serves. Without a word, Jesus got up from the table, removed His outer clothing and wrapped a towel around His waist. After that, He poured water into a basin and began to wash His disciples' feet, drying them with the towel that was wrapped around Him. He said, "Now that I, your Lord and Teacher, have washed your feet, you also should wash one another's feet. I have set you an example that you should do as I have done for you" (John 13:14).

When He had put on His robe and taken His place at the table, He asked His disciples, "Do you understand what I have done for you?" (John 13:12).

Teaching by Example

The key words in our Lord's message are "I have set you an example." Christ not only spoke the truth, but He also lived it. He did not wait until those final hours with His disciples to be an example to them. From the start of His ministry, He served as a model of ministry. The disciples didn't learn their Lord's teachings in a classroom with a pile of textbooks; they learned it in the crucible of daily life as they interacted with people. Jesus was a living example to those who followed Him.

The apostle Peter wrote about the example his Lord set, "To this you were called, because Christ suffered for you, leaving you an example, that you should follow in his steps" (1 Pet. 2:21). This is the theme of Pastor Charles M. Sheldon's classic 1896 novel *In His Steps* written in Topeka, Kansas, and read a chapter at a time to the young people in his church. *Publishers Weekly* reported that for nearly a century, this book had a greater circulation than any other, except for the Bible.

The kind of servant leadership to which our Lord has called us is unnatural—a paradoxical style. On the night in which He was hurting deeply, Christ was well aware that His pain, humiliation and death lay just ahead. He needed the love, support and encouragement of His disciples. But just when He needed them most, His closest and most trusted friend would betray Him, "selling" Him for 30 pieces of silver.

And yet no one ministered to the Lord Christ as this time. Instead, He reached out to them with love, humbly performing the lowliest of tasks—washing their feet (even the feet of Judas, who soon afterward made his move).

Did any of the disciples care? Did they notice what was happening? Probably not. They were discussing instead who was going to sit on Christ's right hand and who on His left in the coming Kingdom. Each made a case for his position, feeling uniquely qualified for that honor. Considering discussions about suffering and death to be distasteful, the Twelve preferred topics focused on the power and glory they would enjoy in Christ's coming kingdom. Minutes later, one of His trusted disciples would betray Him for a few coins.

The kind of servant leadership to which our Lord has called us is unnatural—a paradoxical style.

The disciples' preoccupation with their positions of leadership in the coming kingdom of God was nothing new. Even one of their mothers became involved in the power struggle taking place among the disciples. Were James and John, the sons of Zebedee, too shy to ask to sit on the right and on the left of Christ in His kingdom (see Matt. 20:20-21)? What a request! Did they ask their mother to make the request, thinking it would be more difficult for Jesus to deny the petition of a loving mother?

Jesus' response was, "You don't know what you're asking" (see Matt. 20:22). Then He asked James and John, "Can you drink the cup that I am going to drink?" Without hesitation they replied, "We can!" (see v. 22). Sadly, their eyes were not on Jesus, nor were their hearts in tune with His. They preferred power, prestige and popularity. Naively, they actually believed they deserved such rewards.

Seeking to redirect their minds and hearts, the Lord told His disciples, "You know that the rulers of the Gentiles lord it over them, and their high officials exercise authority over them. Not so with you. Instead, whoever wants to become great among you must be your servant, and whoever wants to be first must be your slave—just as the Son of Man did not come to be served, but to serve, and to give his life as a ransom for many" (Matt. 20:25-28).

As we apply the teachings of our Lord to our own lives and personal situations today, weaker disciples may lose their enthusiasm for the important principles He presented. May we pay close attention to our Lord's teachings on the topic of compassionate, service-minded leadership.

Three Non-negotiable Commands

Shortly before His death, our Lord gave us the following three principles for compassionate leadership that is lived out through charitable service.

1. *To become great, you must be a servant.* Most of us want to be "great," or at least above average. Ever play King of the Mountain when you were a kid? Grownups, too, in one way or another, want to achieve the top spot. Sometimes they use power plays or politics or money or intimidation—whatever they think may be required.

This clawing for the top spot leads many to gossip and slander others, seeking to tear the "competition" down as they build themselves up. In our world, many adults grab power by exerting political pressure or by using their family name or by buying a position by "calling in the chips" from people they've helped in the past. Since this is how the world works, it was natural for James and John to think it might work with Jesus, but it didn't. And it won't work for us today.

How can a person be truly great in the eternal kingdom of God? By becoming humble willing servants.

How can a person be truly great in the eternal kingdom of God? By becoming humble willing servants. Become active in serving Him and others by becoming humble in order to be great in God's kingdom. Humility and servant leadership are linked so much so that humble people, in the end, don't care much about being considered great.

2. *To be first, you must become a servant.* The second divine principle for being "first" is the same as the one for those who wish to become great: Become a servant.

The disciples were privileged characters. They had been chosen by Jesus to belong to an elite group of just twelve men. This privileged status was not lost on these Jews. Without a doubt, they saw themselves as important people within God's kingdom. These men were leaders; they had been selected, enfranchised, trusted with the teachings of God's kingdom.

But these men wanted to be more than merely privileged. Each wanted to be first. James and John, who asked for the privilege, were already in an even more select group of three among the Twelve. Several times in the Gospels we read that James, John and Peter were with Jesus during some notable event. One such event took place on the Mount of Transfiguration. Here James and John tried to ease Peter out and reduce the select company to a twosome. Their strategy was to dispatch their mother who would speak to Jesus and settle things once and for all.

This was a brilliant plan—they would generously leave it up to Jesus to decide who would sit on His right and who would sit on His left. These men must have been convinced that they deserved the place of greatest honor. As brothers, they would "hang together" next to Christ throughout eternity.

That desire for first place, or greatest honor, still creeps into our Christian society. We who have worked with our brother Billy Graham have seen how some pastors and Christian businessmen hang back and do little in the planning stages for citywide crusades, and then maneuver and jockey for position when Mr. Graham arrives in town for preliminary meetings. They want the best seats at luncheons, on the crusade platform, in the public eye.

By contrast, most parents and Christian lay leaders serve quietly and effectively behind the scenes during the months of preparation for a crusade. These types don't think of greatness and aren't concerned about who will gain recognition or who will be in first place. Instead, they simply serve the Lord and others joyfully, as true servant leaders.

3. *To be first, we must follow the example of Jesus.* Our Lord offered to us, by His own conduct, the supreme example of how compassionate servant leaders should act. Imagine the Lord of the universe, Creator of the universe, coming to Earth to minister compassion to all people. He went beyond lowly service and gave His life as a ransom for many (see Matt. 20:28). Other leaders take, but Jesus gave; other leaders had slaves and servants waiting on them, but Jesus had none. He was the "slave" who served.

What an example our Lord has given us. What a powerful statement about Christian leadership. And what a model for us to emulate. He offered two basic choices for Christian disciples: serving and giving.

Serving

This is central to the Christian life: ministering to the authentic needs of people with the love of Jesus Christ and in the power of the Holy Spirit. How do we serve? As our Lord did. He is the perfect example of a servant leader. The apostle Paul wrote to the Philippian Christians that Jesus didn't merely *act* like a servant—no, He *became* a servant (see Phil. 2:5-11).

Giving

Our Lord plainly taught that He came to give His life as a ransom for many. We who follow Him must be willing to do the same—to give ourselves (our very lives, if necessary) for others. John, the beloved disciple, said it this way: "This is how we know what love is: Jesus Christ laid down his life for us. And we ought to lay down our lives for our brothers" (1 John 3:16).

How should this "giving" take place? John goes on to explain: "If anyone has material possessions and sees his brother in need but has no pity on him, how can the love of God be in Him?" He concludes by declaring, "Dear children, let us not love with words or tongue but with actions and in truth" (vv. 17-18).

The servant leader wants to give to others whatever God has given to him or her. The servant leader owns nothing; all he or she has comes from the Lord and is readily available to all who need it. Bob Pierce, founder of World Vision International, took a verse in 2 Chronicles from a Dutch paraphrase that reads: "All that we have comes from God, and we give it out of His hand."

Professor Robert Saucy, a professor at Talbot Theological Seminary in La Mirada, California, gave a splendid description of compassionate living, of servanthood, when he said, "Some talk of a new style of leadership today as involving servant-hood—more collegial, less domineering. Yet there is still a radical difference. . . . Jesus is not talking about taking the role of a servant or a servant leadership style. He is talking about being a servant. The radical difference is that the servant leads totally for the good of other people. The people he leads are his ultimate goal. They are not means to another end."[1]

Our Lord taught this principle clearly when He said, "Give to everyone who asks you, and if anyone takes what belongs to you, do not demand it back. Do to others as you would have them do to you" (Luke 6:30-31). Servant leaders give generously—even as their Lord gives and gives . . . and gives some more.

Regardless of our station in life, God calls all of us as believers to give our best to the Master as com-

> **Regardless of our station in life, God calls all of us to give our best to the Master as compassionate, loving leaders.**

passionate, loving leaders. A brilliant and famous young medical doctor one day grappled with this important decision. During his rise to fame, an urgent call came for him to travel to a village in Korea for a critical operation. At first he refused. "God, my schedule is booked solid for many weeks. How can I go?" But, like the man in the New Testament who said he wouldn't go but did, this surgeon became the chief physician in a Korean missionary hospital.

Some years later, during the visit of a friend, the surgeon asked, "Would you like to see an operation this afternoon?"

"Yes," said his friend, "I would."

For most of that afternoon, the visitor watched from a balcony overlooking the operating table around which a circle of Korean medical students watched intently. As the sun beat upon the tin roof overhead, the surgeon pressed on until five hours had passed and the procedure was complete.

As the surgeon retired from the room, his friend asked, "Is every day like this?" The surgeon only smiled as he wiped the perspiration from his forehead.

"How much will you receive for this?" his friend asked.

The doctor studied the poor Korean woman being wheeled away with only a copper coin in her hand, and then looked back at his friend with tears welling up in his eyes. "Well, sir, for this one I get her gratitude and my Master's smile. But that is worth more than all the profit this world can give."

The Master calls us to be compassionate and giving, to realistically assess our natural and spiritual gifts and to begin investing them in something worth "more than all the profit this world can give."

Note

1. Robert Saucy, quoted in Paul Cedar, *Strength in Servant Leadership* (Waco, TX: Word Books, 1987), p. 85.

THE BIBLICAL MODEL
OF COMPASSIONATE
LEADERSHIP

J esus is our perfect model of compassionate leadership, of leadership that seeks to serve. He is the example we should follow. Christian believers wisely look to Him as their working model whom they can trust, understand and follow.

You'll find compassionate servant leaders everywhere—in the factory, behind the desk, on airplanes, trains, buses and cars. One of them, a young physician named Richard Selzer, visited his public library every Wednesday afternoon to mix it up with elderly men and women who had gathered to read. His story was included in a message on servant leadership delivered by Pastor Bob Kraning at Hume Lake Christian Camps at an autumn retreat.

The doctor's tribe at his library reading room consisted of a core of six regulars and a somewhat less-constant pool of eight others. On very cold days, all eight of them might show up, causing a bit of a jam at the newspaper rack.

One day, as the physician held the front door for a wobbly man in his 80s, the ruddy-faced gent apologized for his gait. "The hinges is rusty," he said, forcing a smile.

"No hurry," the doctor assured him.

But as "Neckerchief" struggled to sit down to read the *Saturday Review*, the old man hissed softly in pain.

"The hinges?" the doctor whispered.

"Nope. The toes," came an explanation.

"What's wrong with your toes?"

"The toenails is too long. I can't get at 'em. I'm walkin' on 'em."

The physician left the library and went to his office, surprising his staff. "I need the toenail cutters," he said. "I'll bring 'em back tomorrow."

In the library, Neckerchief had somehow replaced *Saturday Review* with *U.S. News and World Report*. The physician could only guess what the exchange had cost him.

"Come on down to the men's room," the physician told him. "I want to cut your toenails."

He showed the man his strong clippers that could bite through bone and then led him into one of the booths.

"Don't untie my shoes," the old man cautioned. "I just slide 'em on and off."

After peeling away two pairs of socks, the doctor began to remove those claws. Each big toe looked like the horn of a goat. There was dried blood on each toe. Several people came and went in nearby stalls. *They'll just have to wonder*, the doctor decided.

The procedure took an hour. Occasionally a fragment of nail would fly up and hit the doctor in the face. Afterward, he wet some toilet paper and cleansed the toes, then put the man's socks and shoes back on.

The old man stood up, tested his feet and smiled. "That's a Cadillac of a job," he said. "It don't hurt!" he exclaimed. "How much do I owe ya?"

"On the house," the doctor replied.

Later he trimmed the toenails of "Stovepipe," then of "Mrs. Fringe" (they tied up the ladies' room for half an hour). After that, Doctor Selzer never went to the library on Wednesday mornings without his nail clippers in his briefcase.

"You just never know," said this servant leader.

So why aren't there more leaders like this doctor, more men and women willing to step away from the spotlight and step into the sandals of the Master? Well, for one thing, this whole idea of a compassionate leader seems unnatural; after all, the world does not associate service to others as something a leader usually does.

In fact, being waited on by others—having your every need met—isn't that usually considered a perk that comes with a position of leadership?

The apostle Peter himself struggled with the challenging call to be a leader who serves. But Peter had the advantage of observing compassionate servant leadership, as it was modeled by Jesus as they lived and ministered together.

Several years after Christ's resurrection, when Peter had become one of the most influential leaders of the Early Church, he appealed to the other leaders as "fellow elder[s]" (1 Pet. 5:1). He never wrote from a position of ecclesiastical hierarchy or political power. Instead, he wrote to others as a humble, loving servant of Jesus Christ—as a compassionate leader.

The Compassionate Leader as Shepherd

Peter's first exhortation to Christian leaders was to shepherd the flock of God entrusted to their care (see 1 Pet. 5:2). The term "shepherd" is used synonymously with that of "pastor." And certainly the apostle's original readers were quite familiar with the imagery he was using in his exhortation.

In the early twenty-first century, we use this imagery to reflect the compassionate servant leader who seeks to shepherd God's people. The entire concept of serving as a leader in Christ's kingdom relates to *people* more than to *tasks*. Whatever the ministry might be to which God has entrusted us, we are directed to shepherd the people whom God is calling us to lead.

Of course, there are many other ways to be a servant in addition to being the pastor of a church. Whenever, or however, Christians serve in leadership roles, it is always appropriate to be a servant leader—like Jesus. At the same time, we are to remember that it is God's flock and not ours. They are His people, the sheep of His pasture. We are simply the under-shepherds, or "under-leaders." Jesus Christ is the Chief Shepherd. As under-shepherds, we carry a tremendous responsibility. We are accountable to God for how we lead and nurture those entrusted to our care.

There are many other ways to be a servant in addition to being the pastor of a church.

The apostle James reminds us of this awesome responsibility when he writes, "Not many of you should presume to be teachers, my brothers, because you know that we who teach will be judged more strictly" (Jas. 3:1). Indeed, we as Christian leaders must be careful how we lead our followers, the flock of God. We are accountable to the Chief Shepherd for how we carry out His will.

The Compassionate Leader as Obedient

The apostle Peter then provides a practical working model for us as leaders who seek to serve. His first point is that we should serve "not because you must, but because you are willing, as God wants you to be" (1 Pet. 5:2).

God is not as concerned with what we do as with why we do it. Love, of course, needs to be the basic motive for everything a Christian does, including serving and leading others. Motive is the key. Why are you serving? The moralizers, under a heavy cloak of legalism, serve because they ought to, but theirs is a joyless service.

We should never lead out of a sense of obligation, or because we feel trapped, having no voice in the matter. God invites us to serve willingly, from a joyful heart filled with love and devotion.

The Compassionate Leader as Eagerly Obedient

Peter's second piece of practical advice is that we should be "eager to serve" (1 Pet. 5:2). Not many people are *eager* to be servants, and yet that's just what the Scriptures encourage us to be.

It's more natural for people to volunteer to be leaders for personal gain, yet we who find ourselves in the full-time work of the ministry did not become involved because of the money we would make. Nearly every servant of

A truly compassionate servant leader runs from every temptation.

God today could make more money in other professions. Of course there have been unprincipled con men in the ministry, dishonest in their financial dealings, but these are decidedly in the minority.

A truly compassionate servant leader runs from every temptation to lead for personal gain—whether it's for money, power or prestige.

Stop and ask yourself: "Am I in my leadership role for personal gain? Or do I feel trapped without options?" If either is true, stop reading right here and ask the Lord to forgive you. Repent, and then willingly pick up your shepherd's staff and serve the flock of God without regard to personal recognition.

Robert K. Greenleaf addressed this very issue on the first page of his classic book *On Becoming a Servant Leader*:

The servant-leader is a servant first. It begins with the natural feeling that one wants to serve, to serve first. Then conscious choice brings one to aspire to lead. That person is sharply different from one who is leader first, perhaps because of the need to assuage an unusual power drive or to acquire material possessions. For such it will be a later choice to serve—after leadership is established. The leader-first and the servant-first are two extreme types. Between them there are shadings and blends that are part of the infinite variety of human nature.

The difference manifests itself in the care taken by the servant—first to make sure that other people's highest priority needs are being served. The best test, and the most difficult to administer, is: Do those served grow as persons? Do they, while being served, become healthier, wiser, freer, more autonomous, more likely themselves to become servants?[1]

A minister, seeking the good of those to whom he ministers, must help them to discover their mutual ministry, wrote Clyde Reid.

No longer must he be seen as the one who stands at the center of all the church's activities, head and shoulders above the congregation. Instead he must lose his life as the absolute leader, the one who stands at the center of all activity, head and shoulders above the congregation—in order to find his true life as servant, as the releaser of the ministry of his people. This is an exciting and demanding concept of ministry.[2]

Are you in your leadership role for personal gain? Or can you serve eagerly, without an eye on being paid? Let us repent, if we are not serving the Lord eagerly, with the goal of pleasing Him alone. When leaders are eager, followers reflect that same eagerness. Under normal circumstances, a congregation is the length and shadow of its shepherd. Members reflect the attitude and ministry style of their pastor. When a pastor is eager, so will be the congregation. When the pastor is generous and forward looking, so will his congregation be.

The Compassionate Leader as an Example

Returning to the passage in 1 Peter 5, we see that Peter gives us one more piece of practical advice: "[serve by] not lording it over those entrusted to you, but being examples to the flock" (v. 3). Most leaders tend to lead by asserting their authority—a fact that Jesus pointed out to His disciples. The Gentiles, He said, "lord it over them" and "exercise authority over them" (Matt. 20:25). How do we "lord it over" others? We throw our weight around; we become dictators; we make the plans and expect everyone else to follow.

Pei-Lu Liu, a wonderful Chinese Christian lady, wrote a letter some time ago to a friend in America. It contained a vivid illustration:

> [When] I think of servanthood, I think of light. In ancient China, outdoor lightings were provided by lanterns. Whenever a guest came to visit at night, it was always the servant who carried the lantern and led the way so that the guest might follow and see the path.

Happy is the husband and father who carries the light for his family. He derives his authority not from holding a certain rank, but by performing the ministry of the Spirit. "The consequence of the obedience of all to God, Christ and the Spirit," Hans Küng once said in describing the Church, "is voluntary and mutual submission, the voluntary ministry of all to all, voluntary obedience to the different charisma of others."

Happy is the husband and father who carries the light for his family.

To be examples to the flock, we must seek to follow the Chief Shepherd as Lord of our lives. We must allow the Holy Spirit to fill us with the fruit of the Spirit and to endow us with the gifts of the Spirit that He chooses to entrust to us. We must serve the Lord and His flock willingly and eagerly and be examples who reflect the character of Jesus Christ our Lord.

Eleven Principles of Intelligent Leadership

As we reflect Jesus Christ to others, as we lead as He leads, success will be the natural result. And good leadership ensures success, both on the battlefield and in the boardroom. Intelligent leadership involves common sense, according to the U.S. Marine Corps. The following are 11 principles of responsible leadership that the Marines have formulated and tested during the past 200 years:

1. Take responsibility for your actions and for the actions of your subordinates.
2. Know yourself and seek self-improvement.
3. Set the example for those around you.
4. Develop your subordinates.
5. Ensure that a job is understood, then supervise it and carry it through to completion.
6. Know your people and look after their welfare.
7. Keep everyone informed.
8. Set goals that you can reach.
9. Make sound and timely decisions.
10. Know your job.
11. Develop teamwork among your subordinates.

Notes
1. Robert K. Greenleaf, *On Becoming a Servant Leader* (San Francisco: Jossey-Bass Publishers, 1996), p. 1.
2. Clyde Reid, *Pastoral Psychology*, vol. 19, no. 183 (April 1968), pp. 13-14.

CHAPTER 3

THE PERILS OF
COMPASSIONATE
LEADERSHIP

Compassionate leaders are as susceptible to temptations of the flesh as anyone else. And, of course, our enemy, the Devil, who walks about as a roaring lion, seeking whom he may devour, never misses an opportunity to deceive or lead astray (see 1 Pet. 5:8). Though temptation exists in the realm of the flesh, Satan never fails to exploit areas of weakness in the spirit as well.

"A Proud Look"

Does it matter to God when pride seizes the heart of a successful servant leader? Does He care when that sin causes an individual to put self upon the throne, making God a secondary figure? It's clear from Proverbs 16:5 that "the LORD detests all the proud of heart." Pride is the sin that changed the anointed cherub into a foul fiend of hell.

Pride attacks in many subtle ways, but spiritual pride is the most heinous. To become proud of any spiritual gift is to forget 1 Chronicles 29:16, which reminds us that "all that we have comes from God, and we give it out of his hand." To take pride in our spiritual gifts is to forget that without God, we are nothing and we have nothing but sinful lives.

In Proverbs 6, God plainly tells us that among the seven things He hates are "a proud look, and a lying tongue." Unfortunately, the victim of pride is often the one who is least aware of his sin. Do you want to know how to identify pride when it surfaces in your life? Apply the following tests to determine whether you suffer from pride:

- *The test of humility.* How do you feel when another is selected to fill a position you are abundantly qualified for?

When someone else is promoted? Or when another's gifts seem greater than your own and are acknowledged?

• *The test of motive.* In all honesty, how do you feel when self-reflection reveals problems and weaknesses? Do you face your inadequacies honestly and objectively?

• *The test of criticism.* Can you handle criticism from others? Or do you become resentful and rush to criticize the one who criticizes you?

All pride should end when we measure ourselves against the life of Jesus, who humbled Himself on the cross. A truthful assessment of our own shabbiness, vile temper and proud looks leads us to echo the song of James M. Gray:

> *Boasting excluded, pride I abase;*
> *I'm only a sinner, saved by grace.*[1]

All pride should end when we measure ourselves against the life of Jesus.

Arrogance

The most repulsive manifestation of pride is egotism, the tendency to think and speak of oneself, of magnifying one's attainments, and of relating everything to self rather than to God and God's people. Any leader who has been admired by many followers for many years is in peril of losing perspective and being defeated by the sin of arrogance.

Many years ago, Robert Louis Stevenson told the story of a prophet in Samoa who wore a veil because, he claimed, the radiance of his face was too much for others to look upon. Eventually, the prophet's veil grew ragged and fell off. Then the people discovered that the prophet was only a decrepit old man trying to hide his ugliness.

However persistently a leader might try to hide his blemishes of character, eventually the mask falls away and his true face is revealed. Will people see in you the ugliness of egotism or the transfigured glory of Christ the Lord?

How do you listen to the praises of other people? Until you can hear another leader praised without desiring to belittle his work or praise your own, there is an unmortified mountain of egotism yet to be surrendered and brought under the grace of God.

The Green-Eyed Monster

Suspicion, envy, pride and bitterness are all close relatives of the sin of jealousy. And jealousy is nothing new. Moses faced this temptation when an outraged Joshua—a loyal colleague of Moses'—after hearing that Eldad and Medad were prophesying in the camp, demanded, "Moses, my lord, stop them!" (Num. 11:28).

But the seasoned old patriarch correctly sized up the situation among the assistants he had selected. "Are you jealous for my sake?" Moses asked Joshua. Then Moses went on to declare, "I wish that all the Lord's people were prophets" (Num. 11:29). Envy and jealousy could find no fertile ground in Moses' heart. He was telling his men, "Be encouraged by God's work in others; don't snuff it out."

As Dr. Stan Mooneyham, former president of World Vision, used to say, "It's never safe to play it safe."

Handling Fame

All leaders (including preachers) enjoy being liked by others. Being disliked, of course, is no virtue, but popularity can come at a pretty high price. Jesus knew this. He warned, "Woe to you when all men speak well of you" (Luke 6:26).

Some great spiritual leaders have cultivated personality cults that focus on their special talents, virtues or good looks. Fawning, awestruck followers and deferential crowds become hallmarks of the larger-than-life leader. What's worse is when that leader actually embraces his pedestal, truly believing that he *is* larger than life.

This problem surfaced when the apostle Paul was in Corinth. Christians there were divided into camps, each promoting its favorite personality. Some liked Apollos, others preferred Paul. "Stop it!" Paul demanded. "I planted, Apollos watered, but God caused the growth" (see 1 Cor. 3:6). Further, Paul explained that any devotion or loyalty Corinthians had for their spiritual leaders was misdirected—such devotion and loyalty should be directed solely to the person of the Lord Jesus Christ. Paul knew that spiritual leaders could be held in the "highest regard in love because of their work," but that esteem must not degenerate into adulation (1 Thess. 5:13). Accepting encouragement is no sin, but leaders must refuse to be idolized by the people they serve.

Spurgeon felt the danger of popularity pressing close to his heart.

In a lecture to theological students, Stephen Neill warned that "popularity is the most dangerous spiritual state imaginable, since it leads on so easily to spiritual pride which drowns men in perdition. It is a symptom to be watched with anxiety, since so often it has been purchased at the too heavy price of compromise with the world."[2]

Spurgeon felt the danger of popularity pressing close to his heart.

> Success exposes a man to the pressure of people and thus tempts him to hold on to his gains by means of fleshly methods and practices, and to let himself be ruled wholly by the dictatorial demands of incessant expansion. Success can go to my head, and will unless I remember that it is God who accomplished the work, that He can

continue to do so without any help, and that He will be able to make out with other means whenever He cuts me down to size.[3]

Although George Whitefield was enormously popular as a preacher on America's frontier, he grew tired of the attention as his career progressed. "I have seen enough of popularity to be sick of it," he declared.

The Myth of Man's Infallibility

Although the Spirit-filled person is less likely to make mistakes of judgment than his secular counterpart, perfection eludes us all. Even the apostles made mistakes that required divine correction.

Even though spiritual leaders often give themselves to prayer and to wrestling with the problems of renewal and revival, many find it difficult to concede the possibility of misjudgment or mistake. A willingness to concede error and to submit to one's peers increases one's influence rather than diminishes it. Followers will lose confidence in a leader who appears to believe himself to be infallible.

Indispensability

Even influential Christian workers have fallen before the temptation to consider themselves indispensable. Some older, seasoned believers cling to authority long after it should have passed to younger people.

In a church on the East Coast, a church member in his 90s held tightly to the position of superintendent of his church's Sunday School, even though younger people were able and willing—even eager—to assume his role. Sometimes, well-meaning followers encourage the notion of indispensability, and that feeds the leader's ego, making him less objective about his performance in office. Missionaries need to teach nationals to assume leadership as early as possible.

Riding the Emotional Roller Coaster

The life in Christ includes both frustration and joy. Many leaders swing between the perils of depression and joy. Achieving a balance is not easy. Once when the 70 disciples returned from a mission with great joy, Jesus reminded them not to rejoice about the spirits who had submitted to them. Instead, our Lord reminded them to, "rejoice that your names are written in heaven" (Luke 10:20).

After Elijah had such remarkable success at Mount Carmel, he became so depressed he wanted to die (see 1 Kings 19). Our gracious Lord stepped in to help, prescribing two long sessions of slumber and two nourishing meals. After that, the spiritual lessons were introduced to make a lifetime of difference. After all, his discouragement had been unfounded. Elijah needed to stop and think: Seven thousand faithful Israelites had not yet bowed their knee to Baal. By running away, Elijah would deprive this remnant of leadership they desperately needed.

No one sees all of their ideals and goals for God's work reached 100 percent of the time. Even trusted friends will disappoint us; coveted goals will be unreached; sickness, shortfalls, selfishness and/or depression intervene and must be dealt with.

F. B. Meyer, a vigorous preacher, was an optimist, but he was not spared occasional bouts of despair. He had seen too clearly life's seamy side to be free of disappointment and discouragement.

Charles Spurgeon, the notable British preacher, describes his own struggles with depression in his lecture "The Minister's Fainting Fits":

Before any great achievement, some measure of depression is very usual. . . . Such was my experience when I first became a pastor in London. My success appalled me, and the thought of the career which seemed to open up so far from elating me, cast me into the lowest depth, out of which I muttered my *Miserere* and found no room for a *Gloria in Excelsis*. Who was I that I should continue to lead so great a multitude? I would betake me to my village obscurity, or emigrate to America and find a solitary nest in the backwoods where I might be sufficient for the things that were demanded of me. It was just then the curtain was rising on my lifework, and I dreaded what it might reveal. I hope I was not faithless, but I was timorous and filled with a sense of my own unfitness. . . . This depression comes over me whenever the Lord is preparing a larger blessing for my ministry.[4]

All of us experience seasons when everything goes well. Plans are successful, goals are reached, the Spirit moves, souls are saved, and saints are blessed. When these times came to Robert Murray McCheyne, he would kneel and symbolically place the crown of success on the brow of the Lord, to whom it rightly belonged.[5] Preacher Samuel Chadwick told his people, "If successful, don't crow; if defeated, don't croak."[6]

Feeling Disqualified

No matter how successful a person might be, there is always the possibility of becoming disqualified. The apostle Paul feared it. The prospect of being disapproved lingered ever before him. In 1 Corinthians 9:27 (*KJV*), he described how he brought his body "into subjection" so that having preached to others, he himself would not be a castaway.

The Greek word Paul used which we translate "castaway" is one that refers to metals not suitable for coinage. The refining process took these substandard metals out of the process—they did not survive the test. Just so, a Christian can lose the coveted prize for failure to comply with the rules of the contest.

The apostle Paul believed that the body's passions could disqualify a servant leader as well (see 1 Cor. 6:12-20). He worked toward mastering the body's appetites through disciplined moderation—neither through asceticism on one hand (such as causing oneself harm by denial of basic needs) nor self-indulgence on the other (losing strength through careless diet, for example).

No matter how successful a person might be, there is always the possibility of becoming disqualified.

Servant Leaders Are Happier

Dr. Karl Menninger, founder of the famed Menninger Mental Health Institute, learned that people who give of themselves in service to others are the happiest and healthiest. "Giving money is a very good criterion of a person's mental health," he said. "Generous people are very rarely mentally ill. . . . Stinginess is an illness."

An illustration of this is the story of John D. Rockefeller, Sr. As a young man, he was strong and in good health. By the age of 33, he had made his first million. At 43, he owned the largest business in the world. At 53, he was the richest man on Earth and the world's only billionaire.

To reach these goals, he had bartered his own happiness and health. His weekly income was a million dollars, but his digestion was so bad he could eat only crackers and milk. One of his biographers described him as "a mummy."

John D. Rockefeller, Sr. once confessed that he "wanted to be loved." Lacking in consideration for others, he crushed the helpless into the mire of his lust for bigger profits. On the night his physician told him he could not live for another year, Mr. Rockefeller made a startling discovery: He would be unable to take with him even one of his thin dimes into the next world. His was the despair of a little boy who sees the tide rising to sweep into oblivion all the sandcastles he has been building.

For the first time in his life, Rockefeller recognized that money was something to be shared, not hoarded. Like Scrooge, he lost no time in transforming his money into a vehicle to bless others by establishing the Rockefeller Foundation. It would require a book to describe the benefits that resulted from the many hundreds of millions of dollars he showered on universities, hospitals, churches and millions of underprivileged people.

When the rich man began to think of others, something wonderful occurred. He began to sleep, to eat normally and to enjoy life. At the age of 53, he started to practice God's eternal law: "Give and it shall be given unto you." Rockefeller proved the value of this promise and lived until he was 98 years old.

In a lecture, he said, "Let your question be: 'What shall be the fruits of my career? Shall it be the endowment of hospitals, churches, schools . . . ? Do everything you can for the betterment of your fellow men, and in doing this, you will better enjoy life.'"

This story tells us what compassionate, service-minded leadership does for our mental and physical health, but only Christ can provide sufficient motivation for the right kind of giving. Because we are imperfect, our motives for giving can never become perfectly pure. The closest we come to this is in Christ-motivated giving. When we give, we always get something in return.

John D. Rockefeller, Sr., gave out of his abundance; you might be called upon to give out of penury. Which reward from our heavenly Father do you think will be more coveted?

Notes

1. James M. Gray, "Only a Sinner," http://www.cyberhymnal.org/htm/o/n/onlyasnr.htm (accessed February 2006).
2. Stephen Neill, quoted in *The Record* (March 28, 1947), p. 161.
3. Charles Spurgeon, quoted in Helmut Thieleke, *Encounter with Spurgeon* (Philadelphia, PA: Fortress Press, 1963), n.p.
4. Charles Spurgeon, "The Minister's Fainting Fits," quoted in Thieleke, *Encounter with Spurgeon,* n.p.
5. J. Oswald Sanders, *Spiritual Leadership* (Moody Press), pp. 157-158.
6. Ibid.

DISCOVERING
YOUR LEADERSHIP
SKILLS

Every believer has at least one gift. Some Christians have multiple gifts. Your gifts are a divine bestowal to be used to the glory of God. The various gifts of the Spirit are described in 1 Romans 12, Corinthians 12 and Ephesians 4.

We all belong to the Body of Christ, writes the apostle Paul in Romans 12:4, and in verse 6 he adds, "Since we have gifts that differ according to the grace given to us, each of us is to exercise them accordingly" (*NASB*).

Every organization that exists today began with an individual (man or woman). Some later became movements that accomplished great good. Some degenerated into machines and ended up as monuments. But let's concentrate on the *charismata*—the good and personal gifts God bestows on individuals He chooses. He gives the gifts of prophecy, ministry, teaching, exhorting, ruling and mercy as He wishes.

Some people would give anything they possess to be free of endless responsibility and to remain anonymous. Others are miserable and unfulfilled if they are not right in the very thick of shaping, directing and molding programs—these are the men and women who serve as leaders.

What about these leader types? Is theirs a play for power? An appetite to lord it over others? An ego trip? Not if they are motivated and energized by the Holy Spirit. Just as an artist wants to paint, a musician wants to play an instrument, and an evangelist wants to preach, so the one with the gift of administration wants to give active leadership to a program he believes in.

I (Paul) have learned over the years that although God often gives a single major spiritual gift to one of His servants, He frequently gives multiple gifts. Also, I have come to believe that spiritual gifts are dynamic rather than static. For example, as a pastor, I have witnessed again and again the Lord graciously giving a spiritual gift to a Christian at a specific time for a specific need in the Body of Christ.

Therefore, I believe it is wise not only to ask the question, "What is my spiritual gift?" but also to ask the question, "Lord, what are You calling me to do?" I am convinced that whom the Lord calls, He also gifts accordingly. And whom the Lord gifts, He calls to use those gifts.

How to Determine One's Gift

How can you determine your gifts? First, ask for the guidance of the Holy Spirit. He speaks to God's people. Second, if you are called and gifted with gifts of administration or other leadership gifts, your associates will recognize them and appoint you to positions of authority. Third, the Scriptures offer model leaders as administrators in Moses, Paul, Peter and, of course, our Lord Jesus Himself. Mirror your strengths and weaknesses against their performances and you will see where you excel and where you have weaknesses.

Finally, there should be an assurance in your heart that God has given you the gift of leadership. Notice the phrase "should be." Occasionally, some will be drafted who do not believe they are called to lead. Moses was such an individual. He had little confidence that he could do the job. The apostle Paul was another who felt overwhelmed by the assignment, but working with Barnabas and experiencing the guidance and the empowerment of the Holy Spirit kept him faithfully on track as an evangelist to the end of his life.

But what had to happen first? Paul first had to learn how to serve others—beginning with our Lord. In fact, each of the apostles first became "servants" who led with compassion as they served. In both leadership and administration, we are called to be servants. Our Lord, the greatest leader of all, taught that leadership, by its very essence, is serv-

A leader can become so efficient that there's no room for God to lead.

ing. But remember always to allow for "God room." This is the phrase coined by Bob Pierce, founder of World Vision International. He warned that a leader can become so efficient that there's no room for God to lead, and so the blessing is gone.

The Decisive Leader

Every successful leader has the ability to make decisions accurately, swiftly and compassionately. Indecision might be more comfortable, but habitual delay interferes with the realization of potential and the attainment of goals.

Psychologists tell us that everyone indulges in all kinds of unconscious devices to cover up indecisiveness. Procrastination is one—just not getting around to it. Others include allowing people to sway us from making a final decision or leaving the decision to someone else.

Why is making a decision so painful? One reason is that any decision, large or small, involves the risk of being wrong, and that can be dangerous. It could lead to loss of employment and/or damage to an organization's future. Every decision a leader makes involves an assessment of goals and values, as well as the risks involved. Unless a leader has the courage to take risks, even when the stakes are high, he or she is not cut out for administrative responsibilities.

Making difficult decisions is a heavy burden to bear, but that's what strong leaders must do. The result is usually disaster when a leader is reluctant to face problems that require a decision. Famous last words in the annals of business are "He couldn't make up his mind."

A sense of urgency must be a predominant characteristic of a leadership personality. Clarence Randall, president and chairman of Inland Steel, wrote:

> Some very able and conscientious men never make effective administrators because their approach to difficult problems is judicial in its quality rather than dynamic. They concentrate so exclusively on the necessity for doing the best thing that they end up doing nothing. They lack the urgency required in the fast-moving routine of modern administration. Wise as counselors, they perform an important function in cautioning their impetuous associates against pitfalls that might have been overlooked [but] when left to themselves, will never come up with a positive program of action. In most situations, it is far more important to select one possible plan when several are presented and get on with the job, rather than to prolong the debate until the last thread of doubt about which program is best can be removed.

Never be discouraged because you make mistakes. We all do. And God is a forgiving God. Decision making is an important role in this whole matter of leadership.

Basic Rules of Leadership

Many people with leadership gifts fail to learn the art of delegation. A basic principle of management is that we as leaders ought not to be doing things that others can do as well, or better, than we can. The art of delegation is essential if a leader is to fulfill his or her role successfully. Andrew Carnegie knew it. He said "the great manager is the man who knows how to surround himself with men much abler than himself."[1] That may be hard and quite humbling, but it's quite necessary.

As you prepare to delegate, keep these five questions in mind:

1. *Is there anything I do that someone else can do better?* Am I taking full advantage of the people on my staff or other associates who have more knowledge, background and experience in the detail phase of the work?

2. *Is there anything someone else can do instead of me, even if not quite as well?* (A wise leader once realized that he was "running myself ragged because I was neglecting the 'instead of you' principle." Now, he says, "I limit myself to talking over, rather than taking over, the job.")

3. *Is there anything someone can do at less expense than I can?* Should certain work be handled by the person on the spot, instead of necessitating a trip by you, or by someone whose total salary cost is less than yours, even though the job might take that person twice as long?

4. *Is there anything someone else can do with better timing than I?* A less-than-ideal action taken when it is needed may be more valuable than a delayed, but otherwise perfect, handling of the situation.

5. *Is there anything I can do that will contribute to training and equipping someone else?* This is a very important question, and you may find it worthwhile to set up a special program for that purpose alone, mapping out the year ahead to see how key people can participate more fully, maybe even rotating them in different tasks so that they will be more versatile. If possible, plan ahead for others

to eventually completely take over certain responsibilities. You ought always to have someone in the wings whom you are discipling.

A key word in all this is "entrust." When you delegate, entrust the entire matter to the other person, along with sufficient authority so that he or she can make necessary decisions.

Motivation as Key

To see that work gets done properly and on time, a successful leader motivates the people on his staff. J. C. Penney called it "getting things done through other people."[2]

Here are five means of motivation to help you as a servant leader reach goals through others:

1. *Encouragement.* Most often a leader motivates through encouragement or inspiration.
2. *Participation.* Allow others to share in a task.
3. *Recognition.* This very important tip calls for offering sincere, honest compliments to others when they administrate a task exceptionally well on your behalf.
4. *Praise.* Appropriate praise is like sunshine to the human spirit. People can't grow or flower without it.
5. *Corrosion.* Some occasions will require a more forceful motivating action—one that challenges a person for his or her own good, like iron sharpening iron. This step is less common than the other four indicated, but it is a part of the process.

You can also provide motivation for your staff or associates by (1) arriving on time, or early, each morning; (2) remembering your accountability to God for your actions; (3) setting goals and letting yourself be motivated by them; and (4) keep setting, and reaching for, higher goals.

This last point is very important, so don't forget it! Effective leaders set goals—goals that are reasonable and measurable. Effective leaders also prioritize their goals. And finally, effective leaders have a plan to achieve those goals. After all, God is the great Master Planner who laid out a path for humanity even before the earth was created. Throughout the Bible, God reveals His interest in plans—both His and ours. "Present your plans unto the Lord," says Proverbs 16:3. "Commit and trust them wholly to Him. He will cause your thoughts to become agreeable to His will, and so shall your plans be established and succeed." Again, in Proverbs 16:9 the Scriptures declare that "a man's mind plans his way, but the Lord directs his steps and makes them sure."

Planning is a continuous process. It begins before the action, and then continues for the duration of the project. Think of planning as acting, evaluating and re-planning. Many organizations do not realize that planning can help involve many people in any given process. As a result, a well-managed planning process will motivate those in your organization by making them feel that they are an active, important part of the organization. Further, this increased participation will often spawn a host of new ideas.

Plan Well, End Well

Successful leaders have discovered some interesting side benefits of responsible planning. Planning allows us to master change. Planning forces us to organize our expectations and develop a program to bring them about. Planning is the most effective way to draw out our best thinking, our keenest interest and our most efficient way of achieving maximum growth. And, finally, planning is the intellectual arm of organized growth. Sound strange? Think of it this way: Planning is prologue to everything that is carried out. It should not be the activity of a few, but of every member of the team because it is really the business of us all. Goals are not always reachable, but they can be reset if they are not. An airplane pilot would call it "in-flight corrections."

Planning allows us to master change.

Importance of Communication

When setting goals, you must learn to communicate well. Communication is the work of a leader seeking to create understanding and requires both mental and physical effort. Your failure to communicate properly can result in disaster.

One day a man's car stalled on the highway. A woman stopped and asked if she could help. "Yes," said the stranded motorist, "I'd appreciate a push to get the engine started."

The woman nodded. "I'll be happy to do that," she said.

"I've got an automatic transmission," the stranded driver explained, "so you'll have to get me going at about 30 miles an hour before the engine will kick over."

The woman nodded, and started backing up on the highway. Moments later, the man looked with horror into his rear-view mirror as the woman bore down on him going 30 miles an hour. Obviously, proper communication had been lacking.

I (Paul) learned quite early in my ministry the importance of communicating with others openly and honestly. On one occasion, I was assigned the task of helping a young executive develop some interpersonal skills. Although he was very gifted in administration, he had great difficulty interacting effectively with others.

My boss had given me the assignment secretly. He asked me to come alongside the young man and help him to be more sensitive toward others and more effective in working with them. I soon learned that my assignment was a very difficult one. The young man was extremely abrasive and rude. But as I communicated with him and spent time with him, he seemed to respond well to my suggestions and guidance.

After several weeks of spending time with him, I heard him speaking with one of the girls in the office. He was attempting to pay her a compliment: "My, you look good today. Your dress is so pretty."

I sat back in my chair with a triumphal feeling—until he continued by saying, "Your dress makes you look not so fat."

I quickly learned that I needed to be more clear and less subtle in my communications with him. In fact, there is often a need for "loving confrontation" in our communication with others. We need to learn to be more effective in what the Bible describes as "speaking the truth in love" (Eph. 4:15). I believe that God has given people the ability to deal with truth when it is shared lovingly and constructively. We need to communicate with others clearly and honestly with love, gentleness and sensitivity. I believe that is the very spirit of Jesus.

To some leaders, communication is a one-way process—telling others what they want them to know, think and do. This can be an improper assumption. Many times we fail to make ourselves understood because we frequently mistake the vehicle we use to communicate for the communication itself.

If we want to communicate as true servant leaders, we have to ask ourselves ahead of time: (1) What do I intend really to say or to write? (2) What have I actually said or written? (3) What will the emotional impact be on the person who will read or hear what I have written or said?

Then the following three questions apply to the individuals with whom you desire to communicate: (1) What does the individual expect to hear or read? (2) What will the individual actually read or hear, in spite of what is really spoken or written? (3) How will the person feel about what is read or heard?

Never let the purpose of communication be to impress, but always to communicate.

Never let the purpose of communication be to impress, but always to communicate—not to carry on a semantic handball game, but to make the other individual understand the message. Make sure the message is understood and always convey what is significant to the communicator in terms he or she will understand.

The effective leader is not always the one who can speak and administrate effectively. Sometimes it's the one who can correctly hear and interpret what others are saying. Listen carefully when people speak. Every time people speak they reveal something of themselves to the careful observer. Listening is an essential part of effective communication—and a truly compassionate leader will be a good listener.

Get Excited!

Get excited about your work. Do you enjoy what you are doing? An enthusiastic leader can turn any mundane job into an elevated position. There is nothing that will improve the atmosphere and productivity of an organization, home, church or business like an enthusiastic person who genuinely affirms others. Ask yourself, "Does my presence refresh those who are discouraged?"

Be positive. See positive solutions in every situation. Make every problem a challenge to be overcome. Edward Cole, when he was president of General Motors, was asked, "What makes you different from other men? Why have you moved ahead of thousands of others for the top job at General Motors?" Mr. Cole thought for a moment and then replied, "I love problems."

How about you? Are you overcome by problems? Or do you overcome them? Perhaps it's time to quit speaking the problem and start speaking the solution. Become an encourager. Henrietta Mears, founder of Gospel Light Publications, used to say, "Every time I meet someone I visualize a sign across their chest which says, 'My name is _____. Please help me feel important.'"[3]

Find a Barnabas and Timothy
Every Christian servant leader needs a Barnabas—someone to stand with him in prayer, support and counsel. Every Christian servant leader ought to have a Timothy, one to whom he gives himself, someone with whom he shares.

Be Accountable!
And we believe that every Christian servant leader needs to be part of an accountability group. Both of us feel very strongly about this from personal experience. In fact, we both enjoyed and profited from an accountability group in which we were both involved for the 10 years we lived in the same community.

Compassionate leaders aren't born; they grow— they develop.

Just remember, compassionate leaders aren't born; they grow—they develop. And they reach out to those who need them. They function with joy, bear up well emotionally and are happy serving where God has put them.

Don't Pass the Buck

Soon after God called Moses to servant leadership, the patriarch objected. "Lord," he said, "send, I pray, some other person—someone with more talent and experience than me" (see Exod. 4:10,13). Then we are told that the Lord became angry with Moses but agreed to enlist his brother Aaron the Levite to help Moses (see vv. 14-17).

Although Moses started out in reluctant obedience, God accepted his weakness by asking, "What is that in your hand?" and Moses answered, "A staff" (v. 2).

God said, "Use it."

He asked the same of David, who replied, "A sling." And God said, "Use it."

He asked the apostle Paul, who answered, "A pen." And God said, "Use it."

If God asked you what is in your hand, how would you answer? Whatever you offer, God says, "I'll take what you call nothing and make it something."

Excuses are many: "I simply don't have the time . . ." or "I'm too old . . ." or "I'm too young . . ." or "I'm too inexperienced . . ."

These excuses are not new. Martin Luther was hesitant at first, feeling too modest to preach. John Knox was equally backward about using his gift. When an unexpected request was made of him at the age of 42, he broke down in tears and withdrew to his room. When the Lord called Jeremiah, the prophet replied, "Oh, Lord, I cannot speak for I am only a child" (see Jer. 1:6). Each one of these men had an awareness of their limitations when he was asked to perform a task for his Lord.

Yet even a lack of gifts is never a valid enough reason to refuse when God calls us to servant leadership. God is not primarily interested in enlisting gifted people. Rather, He delights in taking the weak and manifesting His power through them. Our limitations are simply God's opportunities.

"Not that we are sufficient of ourselves to think of anything as being from ourselves," the apostle Paul writes (2 Cor. 3:5, *NKJV*). When he prayed earnestly that limitations be removed, God told him, "My grace is sufficient for you, for My strength is made perfect in weakness" (2 Cor. 12:9, *NKJV*). Therefore Paul could write, "I will boast all the more gladly about my weaknesses, so that Christ's power may rest on me" (2 Cor. 12:9).

Servant leaders who depend upon God become not parasites but people of stature. Never are people as tall as when they kneel before God. When He calls, He equips.

Moses said, "Send someone else," but Isaiah said, "[Lord,] here am I. Send me" (Isa. 6:8).

What do you say?

Notes
1. Andrew Carnegie, "Scots and Scots Descendants in America; Part V—Biographies," *Electric Scotland*. http://www.electricscotland.com/contact.htm (accessed December 5, 2005).
2. J. C. Penney, "On Leadership," *JCPenney.net*. http://www.jcpenney.net/company/history/ history/archive18.htm (accessed December 5, 2005).
3. Henrietta Mears, quoted in Pastor Ray Pritchard, "You've Been Chosen to Clap and Cheer," *Calvary Memorial Church*. http://www.calvarymemorial.com/pastor_ray/sermons/read_sermon.asp?id=292 (accessed December 5, 2005).

COMPASSIONATE LEADERS AND MENTORSHIP

It is rare today when anyone calls another to account for his or her deeds. However, this act of love is beautifully suited to the role of a compassionate servant leader who is fulfilling the role of mentor. No one can ask the hard questions and demand answers as effectively as he or she can.

The term "mentor" first appeared in Greek mythology when Ulysses asked a wise man named Mentor in Homer's *Odyssey* to care for his son, Telemachus, while Ulysses was fighting in the Trojan War. To be sure, the original Mentor had an unfair advantage over his namesakes today. Whenever his duties demanded more than he could handle, the goddess Athena mysteriously appeared, took on his form and lent a hand. The fabled Mentor must have done his job well because Telemachus grew up to be an enterprising lad who gallantly helped his father recover his kingdom.

A mentor today has objectives in the real world that are beyond the stuff of legends. "Discipler" is a close synonym, with these differences: A discipler is one who helps an understudy to (1) give up his or her own will for the will of God the Father; (2) live daily a life of spiritual sacrifice for the glory of Christ; and (3) strive to be consistently obedient to the commands of his Master.

Stages of Accountability

As children grow and mature, they often step away from one of the healthiest situations of their lives—the accountability they had with mom and dad. Just as they reach the critical years of the late teens and early 20s, the young people move into a dormitory hundreds of miles away or get a job in another part of the country or marry and move in with a spouse. By now, the relationship at home that provided consistent accountability is nearly gone.

From that point on, mother and father don't say much, even though they see their children making unwise decisions. After all, parents don't want to appear to be meddling and keeping the children dependent. Young people risk abusing their power unless a mentor is there who loves them enough to tell them the truth.

Problems in making and spending money, stress in their marriage, promotions into situations that offer just enough power for persons to hang themselves—all these can lead to disaster unless the parents, as servant leaders, embrace the role of lifelong mentor and tell their grown children the truth in love.

> **Young people risk abusing their power unless a mentor is there who loves them enough to tell them the truth.**

Accountability in the Bible

Joseph in the house of Potiphar was accountable to Egypt's ruler. Even when Potiphar's wife made those unwise advances on the innocent man and later screamed rape, Joseph was accountable to Potiphar (see Gen. 39:7-20).

When Saul became king, he was in such a hurry for the prophet Samuel to arrive that he himself presented the offering to the Lord and was soundly rebuked later because Saul the king was accountable to Samuel the prophet (see 1 Sam. 13:8-14).

When David scandalized the nation by committing adultery with Bathsheba and by murdering Uriah, Nathan the prophet stood before the king and charged him with the crimes because David the king was accountable to Nathan the prophet (see 2 Sam. 12).

When Nehemiah wanted to travel to Jerusalem and rebuild the city wall, he had to get permission from Artaxerxes because he was accountable to the king for whom he worked as a cup-bearer (see Neh. 2:1-9).

When Daniel had to disobey the king and his colleagues, he remained very much at ease, because he was accountable to God and there was nothing to hide (see Dan. 6).

One of the things that marked the life of our Lord when He came to Earth was His submission to the Father's will. The apostle John tells us on more than one occasion that Jesus always did what pleased the Father (see John 8:29).

To the 12 men whom Jesus had selected to be His disciples, He passed the torch for the work of the ministry. These men were accountable to Him and, ultimately, to each other. Paul and Silas were accountable to the church at Antioch (see Acts 15:35); Onesimus the slave was accountable to Philemon (see v. 10); Timothy was accountable to Paul because the apostle was his father in the faith (see 1 Tim. 1:2).

Mentoring Through Discipline

Some parents are afraid that if they discipline their children, the children think they don't love them. But just the opposite is true. Proverbs 13:24 promises, "He who spares the rod hates his son, but he who loves him is careful to discipline him."

Suzanna Wesley, the mother of John and Charles Wesley, had 11 children. She believed that the self-willed child must have his or her will broken before he or she reaches the age of 2 years. That child must know by then, she believed, that his or her will must yield to the parents' word and authority. One of her 21 principles for child-rearing stated that if ever mentoring needed to be consistent, it is in the mentoring of children. What brought the rod yesterday should bring the rod today.

God wants mentoring parents to create a standard in children. Parents are to be a living example of what is right and what is wrong. If they live out sound moral principles, they will form their children's consciences rightly.

Proverbs 23:13-14 makes a further plea for mentoring with the rod: "Do not withhold discipline from a child; if you punish him with the rod, he will not die. Punish him with the rod and save his soul from death."

When was the last time you took your child by the arm, pulled him (or her) up close and told him what a delight he is to you? It's not fair to discipline only with the tongue. The rod, sandwiched between instruction and correction, is God's way for parents to mentor their children.

Train up a child in the way he should go, and when he is old he will not turn from it (Prov. 22:6).

CHAPTER SIX

OUR
ACCOUNTABILITY
TO GOD

What happens when a servant leader chooses to lead with styles other than that of a loving, caring shepherd? Does it matter to us? Does it matter to God? The answer is an emphatic *Yes!*

Integrity is an outgrowth of a personal or corporate process that reveals what is in our hearts. Each of us makes choices depending upon what the heart dictates. Character is developed by repeating those choices. A series of repetitive choices forms our reputation and determines how we are viewed by outsiders. "One's character lies deeper than values and far deeper than philosophies, allegiances, memberships or accomplishments," said Christian apologist Os Guinness.[1]

Sometimes this becomes more than theory. A well-respected Christian man once served on the board of a nonprofit agency. The president had been accused of sexual harassment and financial misappropriation. The question was, Would the board member be true to his convictions? Would he be the *real* man he so often demanded of other Christians? Sadly, he let the matter slide under the rug. Integrity means doing the right thing, even when it hurts.

The missteps of leaders with strong convictions are often overlooked because they're visionaries; they have big churches; they lead successful ministries. The secret code is, Protect people at the top or too much damage will be done.

This approach must be rejected. Not every decision will be the right one, of course, but taking action means being who we are and emanates from strength of character, rather than from weakness or insecurity.

Obstacles to Character Building

Don Otis, president of Creative Resources, a Christian consulting firm, calls integrity the virtue that our culture lacks and what Christian people "desperately need." In the magazine *Christian Management Report*, he wrote, "Integrity is part of a personal or corporate process that begins with what's in our hearts" where choices are made and where character is developed.[2]

Integrity tolerates dissent. We don't need to have people around us who are always negative, but each of us must listen to the concerns and criticisms of those we lead. A leader must discern between reasonable dissent and fault-finding negativism that can be toxic. Peter Drucker, an expert on management, believed that "any organization needs its nonconformist."[3] He thought that organizations become defective when important decisions are made unilaterally without open discussion.

> **The only antidote for pride is its exact opposite: humility.**

Integrity admits flaws in leadership. Most of us are prepared to acknowledge that we are flawed children of dust, "and feeble as frail," as the hymn goes.[4] We, as Christians, must humbly admit that we don't have the answers to every question that assails us on a daily basis. We make mistakes, cause hurt, and miss opportunities. There isn't a man or woman among us without character flaws, imperfections and fear. After all, Thomas doubted his Savior, Moses murdered a fellow citizen, Elijah ran away from duty, Jonah hid, and David fell into moral sin. However, these men were not defined by what they did wrong, but by what they did right.

Integrity acknowledges our pride. "Pride," wrote C. S. Lewis, "leads to every other vice. . . . For Pride is spiritual cancer: it eats up the very possibility of love, or contentment, or even common sense."[5] Pride is hard for any of us to detect in ourselves. It blinds us to the way people actually see us. The only antidote for pride is its exact opposite: humility.

Think back to the story of Jehoshaphat, king of Judah. Remember what this wise man did when he was informed that a vast army was coming against him? He made four strategic decisions: (1) he inquired of the Lord; (2) he proclaimed a fast; (3) he came together with the people; and (4) he sought help from the Lord (see 2 Chron. 20:1-12). Humility was Jehoshaphat's strength. The king admitted in his prayer, "We don't know what to do, but our eyes are upon you" (v. 12). Jehoshaphat reminds us that there's nothing wrong in admitting that we don't have all the answers.

Integrity leads us to trust in God. Insecurity comes from fear. We all experience fear when we lack the important character quality of trust. Insecure leaders get mad, try to control or intimidate—and that all leads to corporate dysfunction. "Trust in the LORD with all your heart," say the Proverbs, "and lean not to your own understanding" (3:5). Reliance on the Lord and other people is not an admission of weakness. Rather, it is a wise recognition of our own dependence.

Integrity cultivates thanksgiving. God dwells in a thankful heart. When we sinners recognize our weakness in some area of life that we cannot fix on our own, we turn with grateful hearts to the Lord. The key to success here is practice. God established feasts and celebrations as reminders of what He did for His people. A leader who is self-centered is seldom grateful. Instead, he takes credit for his own success and withholds praise from others who deserve it.

Integrity never manipulates unfairly. We can hardly be manipulative and humble at the same time. Oftentimes we seek manipulation and control as a way to deflect attention from our own insecurities. We're afraid to betray flaws in our character. But an honest assessment of our shortcomings will allow us, in humility, to be servant leaders who always make integrity a party to our dealings with others.

Integrity mirrors emotional intelligence. People in leadership some-times struggle with emotional weaknesses that paralyze them. This can turn them into paranoid tyrants. Frustration and failure in leadership are often linked to low emotional intelligence. One can seem to be more competent, more confident and more skilled than most, but people who follow are forgiving if it's proven they are not. They are so confident in a leader's integrity that they will over-look mistakes.

Integrity helps us embrace weaknesses. Acknowledging our weak-ness does not mean that we capitulate to it. Jesus our Lord tells us that His strength is made perfect in our weaknesses (see 2 Cor. 12:9). This is a paradox, but the essence of Christian faith is to trust God to help us rise above our human frailty. He delights in refin-ing us so that we can make a difference in His world.

We can embrace weaknesses as proof that we are unworthy of our leadership position, as the apostle Paul did. As servant leaders we recognize that we are fallible. The sooner this is acknowledged, the more genuine men and women of compassion we will be.

Integrity places people above projects. No visionary leader wants to hear that his project isn't as important as the people who make it happen. Christian workers tend to believe that the ends justify the means. Results are valued, quality sometimes undervalued—as if God's work supersedes our requirement to love people as Christ did.

How can a compassionate leader maintain integrity in his dealings with others? The surest way is to look at how Christ treated them. He was patient, investing enormous energy in peo-ple He met—people we might be tempted to say didn't matter all that much in His mission.

How can you tell whether or not you have integrity in relation-ships? To find the answer, pay attention to how you treat people who are in no position to advance your projects or reputation.

A servant leader is not tempted to fudge the truth or to hide embarrassing facts or to make excuses or rationalize or justify or compromise, because he is "doing it for the Lord." Character wins, and it speaks volumes about the kind of people we are who follow Jesus Christ our Lord.

Dealing with Bad Leaders

Does it matter to God when Christian leaders choose to lead in styles other than that of a loving, caring shepherd? Most emphatically, *yes*. God cares when compassionate leaders lose their compassion, becoming selfish or corrupted with money or power, becoming dictators or deciding to rule like the Gentiles did. Our Savior wants servant leaders to care for His sheep.

> **A servant leader is not tempted to fudge the truth or to hide embarrassing facts.**

In Ezekiel 34, which recounts a prophecy God gave to Ezekiel, almighty God expressed deep concern about the care of His people by outlining 11 divine charges of inadequate rule.

1. *"Woe to the shepherds . . . who take care of only themselves" (Ezek. 34:2)*. This message resembles Christ's warning to Peter when He calls him not to tend the flock of God only for personal gain (see John 21:15). God has not called us to the ministry of taking care of ourselves. Instead, He has entrusted some of His precious people to our care. They are His people—the sheep of His pasture.

Ezekiel wrote about shepherds who had first taken wonderful care of themselves: They had eaten the curds of the sheep's milk, had clothed themselves with the wool of the sheep, and had slaughtered the best of the sheep for their own nourishment (see v. 3). In other words, they had used the sheep for their own benefit.

They cared little about giving, only about receiving. They had become selfish in their role as shepherds, exploiting the people for personal gain but giving nothing in return.

That was not the only sin that God imputed to those shepherds in His prophetic message. Another major sin was strongly implied— the shepherds had taken care of only themselves. By doing so, they had been totally neglecting the needs of their sheep. They had not been providing for the persons whom the Lord had put under their care.

We should love and care for the needy with a generous, service-minded heart.

Evidently, those shepherds thought God wouldn't notice. They had been deceived by their sin. They had become so totally absorbed in doing their own thing and caring for themselves that they had not only completely forgotten their sheep, but they had also forgotten God.

2. *"You have not strengthened the weak" (v. 4)*. The Lord pointed out some of the specific failures of His shepherds. First, He accused them of not strengthening the weak. Every flock will include weaker members who require special care and attention. Every compassionate leader realizes that he or she will never lead a group of people who are totally strong. The weak are always with us. In fact, every church congregation has them. A few require extra time and attention from a pastor, who should love and care for the needy with a generous, service-minded heart.

3. *"You have not . . . healed the sick" (v. 4)*. Healing is a ministry we normally assign to physicians and hospitals; however, we as compassionate leaders are responsible for the healing needs of those we are called to lead. James shared this message when he wrote, "Is any one of you sick? He should call the elders of the church to pray over him and anoint him with oil in the name

of the Lord. And the prayer offered in faith will make the sick person well; the Lord will raise him up" (Jas. 5:14-15).

The Lord is the source of all healing. Neither of these passages suggests that we should not go to doctors or take medicine or have surgery. However, the Scriptures do teach that the servant leader has been entrusted with a healing ministry. It is always right for us to pray for the sick—and then leave the results to God.

4. *"You have not . . . bound up the injured" (v. 4)*. The Lord scolded the shepherds for not binding up the sheep that had been injured. It is a word picture like that of the parable of the Good Samaritan (see Luke 10:25-37). The priest who passed by did not stop to help the injured man, nor did the Levite. Both were religious leaders. Both should have been compassionate leaders, men who served the Lord.

But neither of them stopped to bind up the wounds of the injured man. Perhaps they felt they were too busy. Or maybe they were frightened at the prospect of being beaten and robbed themselves. Or there may have been another reason for their failure to help—the very reason God shared through the prophet Ezekiel. Maybe they were so preoccupied with themselves that they simply ignored those who were hurting—their agenda for the day simply did not include an injured, hurting person.

This is a warning to those of us who have been called to compassionate, service-minded leadership. Like the Good Samaritan, whose only apparent agenda was to respond to an injured man, let us take pity on the needy, bandage their wounds and take care of them until the wounds are healed. This teaching of our Lord is the very foundation of our Christian lifestyle and the very heart of servant leadership.

5. *"You have not brought back the strays" (v. 4)*. Good shepherds watch over their flocks carefully and faithfully, taking care that

none should stray. If there are strays, that is an indictment of the shepherd. Good shepherds know their sheep by name and their sheep recognize the voice of their shepherd and stay close to him or her. Good shepherds lead their sheep to make certain they are safe.

Some elders in a Southern California church one time decided they would "clean up" their church's membership roll by dropping the name of every member they couldn't locate. This deeply troubled the pastor who was able to persuade his zealous elders to organize instead a ministry focused on finding the "strays"— then to go out after them with the love, compassion and patience of the Good Shepherd. Once located, those strays received the help and services they needed within the Body of Christ. If God had led them to another flock, then the church would joyfully release them. But even that could be done only after the church had found them and loved them and cared for them.

6. *"You have not. . . searched for the lost" (v. 4).* Before His ascension, Jesus gave to us what is often called the Great Commission. He instructed all His followers to make disciples of all people. In the course of His ministry, Christ made it clear to all servant leaders that He had come to seek and to save those who were lost (see Luke 19:10).

This is the message of the parable Jesus told about a shepherd who had 100 sheep (see Luke 15:1-7). Ninety-nine of them were safe in the fold; only one was lost. That shepherd left the 99 in the safety of open range while he searched for the lone lost sheep. And when he found it, he joyfully put it on his shoulders and took it home. Then he called his friends for a celebration, saying, "Rejoice with me. I have found my lost sheep" (v. 6). This message is the good news of salvation: Jesus has come to find the lost and to rescue them and to give them eternal life.

7. *"You have ruled them harshly and brutally" (v. 4).* The shepherds had not only neglected the sheep by not strengthening the weak, healing the sick, binding up the injured, failing to bring back the strays and searching for the lost, they had also been guilty of ruling them harshly and brutalizing them. How tragic!

Most of us recoil at the very thought of such treatment of sheep or of any other animal. But we are even more justifiably troubled by the thought of person abuse. We live in a day when the sins of child, wife and even husband abuse are communicated to us regularly in the newspaper and on radio and television. What a tragic indictment those sins are on our society.

But God was actually accusing His shepherds of being guilty of the horrible sin of abusing His sheep by, first, treating them harshly. Those of us who are parents need to guard against this sin. Christian parents who are servant leaders must treat their children with love, respect, tenderness and gentleness—as Jesus would do.

The apostle Paul warns Christian fathers not to provoke or exasperate their children (see Eph. 6:4). Instead, we should bring our children up in the nurture and instruction of the Lord. In other words, we should treat our children just as the Lord would treat them. In fact, it is important for Christian parents to recognize that we are only the under-parents (or under-shepherds) of our children. If we are serious about following Jesus as Lord, we have given our children to Christ along with everything else we have in our possession. It is both awesome and freeing to know that we are caring for the Lord's children.

Of course, that realization is helpful to us as we contemplate our role as servant leaders who model compassion. We care for the Lord's people. They are never our own. We are merely overseers who are tending the flock of God entrusted to our care.

Second, these shepherds were guilty of treating their sheep brutally. It is one thing to be harsh (verbal and emotional abuse), but when we speak of brutality, we are usually referring to actual physical abuse. Can you imagine a shepherd of God abusing the sheep in any way—emotionally, spiritually, physically or even sexually? It should never be so.

8. *You have scattered the flock (see v. 5)*. Next, the Lord accused His shepherds of being responsible for scattering His flock. "So they were scattered because there was no shepherd, and when they were scattered, they became food for all the wild animals" (v. 5). That is what happens when a servant leader forsakes his flock. First, the people scatter, because they do not know what to do or where to go. The biblical description of these hurting and disoriented people is intensely graphic—they are like sheep "without a shepherd." That is the ultimate description of helplessness. And it is the description of many people in our society—even in our churches—who need compassionate, service-minded men and women to lead them.

9. *God is against such shepherds (see v. 10)*. Can you think of anything more terrible than having God against you? What a contrast this statement is to that of the apostle Paul when he declared, "If God is for us, who can be against us?" (Rom. 8:31).

To state the matter bluntly, these shepherds had become traitors. They had changed sides. They were no longer on God's side; they had moved to the side of sin by doing their own thing and going their own way. God was on one side, and they were on the other.

10. *God will hold such shepherds accountable for His flock (see v.10)*. "Accountability" is not a popular word in our world, yet God still demands it of any who will be leaders in His kingdom. As we have seen, that is what James meant when he contended that those

who teach will be judged with greater strictness (see Jas. 3:1).

Jesus' parable of the talents also attests to this fact. In His concluding remarks on this parable, Jesus stated this truth in another way: "From everyone who has been given much, much will be demanded; and from the one who has **Servant leaders** been entrusted with much, much more will be **are accountable to** asked" (Luke 12:48). God demands account- **God ultimately.** ability from us, His servant leaders. We must give an account of what we have done with what He has given to us—including the honored role of being leaders in His kingdom.

Paul taught this truth clearly to the Christians at Corinth when he wrote, "So then, men ought to regard us as servants of Christ and as those entrusted with the secret things of God. Now it is required that those who have been given a trust must prove faithful" (1 Cor. 4:1-2). Servant leaders are accountable to God ultimately. And He will hold us accountable for how we have led and cared for His people.

11. *"I will remove them from tending the flock" (v. 10).* Finally, God said that He would remove such shepherds from tending His flock. Once again we are reminded of the basic fact that it is His flock, and He is in charge. If we fail to care adequately for the people of God, He will remove us from leadership.

That is an awesome statement. Many would ask, "How does God remove His leaders from tending His flock?" That is God's business. He does it as He wishes to do it. Both of us (Ted and Paul) have lived long enough to observe the Lord in this awesome activity of removing leaders from roles that they have neglected and/or abused. Sometimes we have seen a bishop or district superintendent remove a pastor from an assigned ministry. Other times, we have seen a Christian executive lose his job or a Christian father lose his family. We all have witnessed the ultimate removal of a leader—death.

Many might object to the very mention of the ultimate punishment, but God is God! He cares for His sheep. He has promised to rescue His sheep and to look after them (see vv. 10-11). He will do so regardless of our failures or objections. He is the Good Shepherd who cares for His sheep.

Keep Running the Race

When our Lord Jesus was at the peak of His ministry on Earth, He drew crowds of happy people. But when He began losing favor with authorities and was arrested, they deserted Him. The apostle Paul warns servant leaders today, "Let us not get tired of doing what is right, for after a while we will reap a harvest of blessing if we don't get discouraged and give up" (Gal. 6:9).

Sports heroes know the psychology of winning. Tom Landry, coach of the Texas Cowboys and the "winningest" coach in football, once said: "A champion is simply one who didn't give up when he wanted to." And the apostle Paul likened the race of a Christian to that of competing in sports. "Forgetting what is behind," he wrote in Philippians 3:13-14, "and straining toward what is ahead, I press on toward the goal to win the prize for which God has called me heavenward in Christ Jesus."

Our Lord reached His goal by paying the price—He reached it by establishing a Kingdom like no other—not by force or compulsion, not by scepter or sword, not by crushing authority or a reign of occupation. No, He did it by laying down His life. Who could have imagined that His meekness could establish a Kingdom that would overcome the forces of evil and last forever? He said, "I am the good shepherd. The good shepherd lays down his life for the sheep. . . . No one takes [my life] from me, but I lay it down of my own accord" (John 10:11,18).

As a servant leader, Christ humbled Himself, going so far as to die on a cross, like the worst of criminals. And because of it, "Every knee should bow, in heaven and on earth and under the earth, and every tongue shall confess that Jesus Christ is Lord, to the glory of God the Father" (Phil. 2:8).

Notes

1. Os Guinness, *Character Counts* (Grand Rapids, MI: Baker Books, 1999), p. 12.
2. Don Otis, "Roadblocks to Integrity: Potholes to Dodge in Building Character," *Christian Management Report*, April 2004, p. 1. http://content.silas partners.com/383/42427/383_42427_April04CMR.otis.pdf (accessed February 22, 2006).
3. Peter Drucker, *The Drucker Foundation Self-Assessment Tool: Participant Workbook* (San Francisco: Jossey-Bass, 1999). http://www.pfdf.org/leaderbooks/sat/questions.html (accessed December 6, 2005).
4. Robert Grant, "O Worship the King." http://www.cyberhymnal.org/htm/o/w/owtking.htm (accessed February 22, 2006).
5. C. S. Lewis, *Mere Christianity* (San Francisco: HarperSanFrancisco, 2001), n.p. http://www.a.ghinn.btinternet.co.uk/greatsin.htm (accessed December 6, 2005).

COMPASSIONATE LEADERS AND FOLLOWERS

If we are to obey our Lord as compassionate servant leaders, we must become active participants of His Body—the Church. This requires that we become servants of Christ and servants of one another as well.

Some Christians are called to be leaders, but all Christians are called to be followers. In fact, most of us are called to be both leaders *and* followers, but most people don't want to be followers. Seemingly many of us want to be leaders. In our society, we like to do our own thing. We long to be captain of our ship, master of our own destiny.

Does our Lord direct us to follow our own instincts? He says that we must *deny* ourselves, take up our cross and follow Him (see Mark 8:34). We enjoy satisfying our appetites, but God tells us to beat our bodies into subjection so that we can serve Him (1 Cor. 9:27).

One of the true tests of our qualifications to be effective servant leaders is whether we are willing to become true servant followers. We first follow Jesus Christ as Lord, and then we follow those whom God has designated as our human leaders.

The Word of God gives us our instructions for being good followers. For example, in the closing words of Paul's first letter to the Corinthian church, he referred to the household of Stephanas the first converts in Achaia. He described those church leaders as people who "devoted themselves to the service of the saints" (16:15). In other words, Paul implies that they did not merely serve the saints passively; rather, they served actively and were vivid examples of servant leaders.

The apostle Paul instructed the Corinthian believers to submit themselves to those leaders and to everyone who joins in the work (see 1 Cor. 16:16). He then spoke about Stephanas, Fortunatus and

Achaicus who had come to visit him with supplies. By doing so, they had greatly encouraged Paul and had refreshed his spirit. Paul concludes, "Such men deserve recognition" (1 Cor. 16:18). Paul seems to be making it clear here that recognition is due those servant leaders in the church who have been called of God and have been anointed by the Holy Spirit. We are to recognize and accept their authority.

The author of the book of Hebrews wrote, "Remember your leaders, who spoke the word of God to you. Consider the outcome of their way of life and imitate their faith" (13:7). This teaching, addressed specifically to followers, parallels that of Paul, written from a leader's perspective, when he wrote, "Follow my example, as I follow the example of Christ" (1 Cor. 11:1).

Principles of Leadership

The author of the epistle to the Hebrews called readers to "obey your leaders and submit to their authority. They keep watch over you as men who must give an account. Obey them so that their work will be a joy, not a burden, for that would be of no advantage to you" (Heb. 13:17). This passage reveals several important principles of leading and following in the kingdom of God.

"Obey your leaders." First, the scriptures make it clear that obedience is the key to Christian discipleship. Few committed Christians would deny that we are expected to obey God in all that we do. Jesus said, "If anyone loves me, he will obey my teaching. My Father will love him, and we will come to him and make our home with him. He who does not love me will not obey my teaching" (John 14:23-24). So when we obey Christ, He and the Father actively abide in us in the Person of the Holy Spirit. Jesus said, "But you know him, for he lives with you and will be in you" (v. 17).

Obedience to God releases the presence and the power of the Holy Spirit in our lives. As we have seen, along with the Holy Spirit comes the fruit of the Spirit, including "love, joy, peace, patience, kindness, goodness, faithfulness, gentleness and self control" (Gal. 5:22-23). All of these are wonderful fringe benefits of the life of obedience.

But we need to obey for other important reasons as well. We prove our love for Christ when we obey Him. It is not enough to merely tell Him that we love Him or even to sing beautiful hymns expressing our love for Him. The proof of our love for Christ is our obedience to His commands.

Obedience to God releases the presence and the power of the Holy Spirit in our lives.

And the life of obedience also extends to the leaders whom God has placed in our lives. God tells us that we *should obey those leaders* as they point us toward the life of obedience to Christ. It is not a matter of blindly obeying, but of obeying the Lord who called them to be our leaders in His kingdom.

"Submit to their authority." Obedience is a great challenge for all of us. But the Word of God now proceeds to tell us that we should submit to the authority of these servant leaders. Within our society, we soften the word "obedience" so that it becomes more palatable. No one likes to submit! And few like authority.

But God instructs us to submit to our leaders. This is more than the "mutual submission" we read about in Ephesians 5:21. This is real, honest-to-goodness submission that takes place because these leaders have been given authority over us by God Himself.

"They keep watch over you." One of the functions of a compassionate, service-minded leader is to keep watch over those

entrusted to his or her care. Like a good shepherd watching over his sheep, the servant-leader keeps watch over the people of God.

For some of us, that is a comforting and encouraging statement. It is wonderful to know that we, as God's under-shepherds, care for others. When they are sick or lonely, or when they are facing a need, they can always call on us, knowing that we will care for them. God's people can always come to us for help.

To be true disciples of Jesus, we are told that we must deny ourselves, take up our cross and follow Him (see Mark 8:34). Of course, that demands a great deal of commitment and obedience. And, if we are to obey the Lord, we must become active participants in His Body—the Church. This requires that we become servants of Christ and servants of one another. Each of us uses our spiritual gifts to serve one another and to build one another up in Christian maturity.

"[They] must give an account." As indicated earlier, all of us in God's family are accountable. As certainly as followers are accountable to obey their servant leaders and to submit to their authority, so are the servant leaders accountable to God for how they care for the persons entrusted to them. It is a great privilege to be a servant leader; it is also an awesome responsibility.

This teaching reminds us of the parable of the talents (see Matt. 25:14-30). Jesus told of a master who gave one of his servants one talent, another servant two talents and another five talents. He assumed that each would invest his talents wisely. But when he returned from his business trip, he received only a mixed response. He was pleased to find that the servant with two talents had doubled his investment so that he was able to present the master with four talents. The servant with five talents had also doubled his investment. The delighted master said to both of those servants, "Well done, good and faithful servant! You have been faithful with a few things; I will put you in charge of many things. Come and share your master's happiness" (vv. 21, 23).

However, instead of investing his talent, the last servant had buried it. What was the master's response? "Take the talent from him and give it to the one who has the ten talents. . . . And throw that worthless servant outside, into the darkness, where there will be weeping and gnashing of teeth" (vv. 28,30).

The truths of that parable relate strongly to the teaching of the book of Hebrews. All servant leaders will someday appear before their Master to give an account of their stewardship of the lives of the people over whom they have been given leadership. Servant leaders must give an account to God.

"[Let] their work . . . be a joy." The writer of Hebrews again appeals to the followers to obey their leaders "so that their work will be a joy." What a practical and delightful teaching.

When a follower becomes a burden to a leader, everyone loses.

Every babysitter has youngsters under his or her care whom he or she enjoys—as well as children who disobey, who talk back, who become a burden. The first type of child is pure joy; the second type is tedious. Such children make life miserable for everyone. What a difference obedience or disobedience can make in the life of a babysitter—and a servant leader.

"That would be of no advantage to you." When a follower becomes a burden to a leader, everyone loses. No one wins. The author of Hebrews shares it this way: "Obey them so that their work will be a joy, not a burden, for that would be of no advantage to you" (v. 17). When the people of God obey their servant leaders who love them and who are committed to

watching over them and to building them up, there is an atmosphere of joy and blessing.

Winning God's Approval

As leaders we are often tempted to desire the approval of other people—especially those who are following our leadership. Parents deal with this temptation constantly, as do pastors, teachers and Christian employers. Paul faced that concern in his relationship with the Christians in Galatia. He wrote to them, "Am I now trying to win the approval of men, or of God? Or am I trying to please men? If I were still trying to please men, I would not be a servant of Christ" (Gal. 1:10).

The apostle Paul had a remarkable ability to cut through an issue to expose the heart of the problem. The people in the churches of Galatia were being led astray by false teachers. They were being influenced by leaders who were not servant leaders of Jesus Christ. Instead, those leaders had their own agendas. They were concerned about building their own kingdoms. Paul called the Galatian Christians back to God and back to truth. He exerted his responsibility as their compassionate leader. He loved them. He had founded their churches. He had led most of them to personal faith in Christ. And he was not going to let them be led astray by false shepherds.

As he addressed them very directly and disciplined them verbally, he reestablished his credentials as a servant leader. First, he demonstrated that he was not attempting to win the approval of people by compromising the truth. Instead, he was concerned about winning the approval of God.

Second, he contended that he was not concerned with attempting to please men. In fact, he reminded them that if this were his purpose, he could not be a servant of Jesus Christ. His point was an important one—we cannot function as true servants of Jesus Christ if we are seeking to please people or win their approval. We need to go back to the basic teaching of Jesus when He declared that we cannot serve two masters (see Matt. 6:24).

It is the ultimate purpose of servant leaders to love the people who are following them, to encourage them to follow Jesus and to build them up so that they become spiritually mature. This is exactly what Paul was willing to do for the Galatian Christians. He knew that his greatest gift to them would be to teach them the truth—to call them to accountability. His greatest act of love would be to tell them when they were going the wrong way and to call them back to Jesus. His most important credential was that he was a servant of Jesus Christ. He would not give that up for anybody or anything—not even for the approval of the Galatians.

What a lesson this is for us to learn—to understand that our highest calling and our greatest achievement in life is to be a servant of Jesus Christ. Paul introduced himself as a servant of Jesus Christ in most of his epistles. And so did Peter and James. And so should we.

CHAPTER 8

A NEW GENERATION

OF COMPASSIONATE

LEADERS

Our heavenly Father never coerces anyone to become a member of His family, never forces anyone to enroll for service and never compels a disciple to become a servant leader who embodies compassion. Just as He invited the rich young ruler to enter His kingdom, He gave him the opportunity to accept or refuse His invitation. Unfortunately, the young man decided that he loved his money too much to give it up. He was a servant, or slave, of his money. His life demonstrated the teaching that we can't serve two masters, as he refused Jesus' invitation and walked away from the Savior (see Mark 10:17-23).

Some committed believers today want it all. They are turned off by programmatic thinking and watered-down preaching in many churches. Anthony B. Bradley, a research associate at the Acton Institute for the Study of Religion and Liberty in Grand Rapids, Michigan, says that this new generation of evangelicals is "forging a new breed of followers of Jesus Christ."[1] They call their gathering "Doubt Night," where no questions are inappropriate or too hard to tackle.[2]

A New Period

The rise of young pastors like Mr. Bell and others of his generation represents "a new period in evangelical history," says Robert Webber, author of *The Younger Evangelicals: Facing the Challenges of the New World.*

Mr. Webber, a former Wheaton College professor, distinguishes between "traditional" evangelicals who came of age between 1950 and 1970, the program-based evangelicals of the 1975-2000 era, and a new generation of younger evangelicals beginning around 2000. The new leaders see themselves connected to a lost generation: Many young people flocking to these new churches are reacting against the perceived failures and shortcomings of the baby boomers—their parents, by and large.

With baby boomers, observes Mr. Webber, "came the rise of crime, the inhabitability of the inner cities, the disruption of social institutions, the decline of marriages, the rise of divorce, out-of-wedlock births, the breakdown of values, the suspicion of institutions, the intensification of individualism, the demise of authority, and in general the collapse of modern society as we know it." Baby-boomer misadventures produced collateral damage: the broken and wounded hearts of Gen-Xers and Millennials (born after 1982).

This is "the first generation raised without parents and by the media, i.e., MTV, HBO, etc.," explains Ethan Burmeister, 31, pastor of Core Community in Omaha, Nebraska. "We are a latch-key, street-smart, materialistically saturated, authority-hating, media-induced generation."

Ron Wheeler, 27, pastor of The Gathering in Mt. Vernon, Wash., says, "Xers and Millennials are the recipients of the wealth that their boomer parents amassed. Children were usually spared no luxury. Having very often grown up in a dysfunctional home environment, young people learned quickly how to use the guilty conscience of parents to obtain material substitutes for real intimacy and stability. Ultimately, we are hedonists who, like most spoiled brats, hate the fact that nothing feels real and suffer from a lack of direction and purpose."

A New Approach

Younger evangelicals sensed they needed new ministry methods. "Pragmatic evangelical churches develop programs based on a target group and felt needs," says Bill Clem, 48, a church planter with Doxa in Seattle, Wash. "This really means a church is at the mercy of trends for programming, and that there is an extreme urgency to be tragically hip."

These pastors lament that commercialism and consumerism now dominate evangelicalism. It has become common, they say, for churches to engage in intensive marketing and targeting of people, in an attempt to act as vendors of religious goods and services, much like a Wal-Mart or Target. "We're just peddling spiritual goods and services instead," says The Gathering's Mr. Wheeler.

Eric Stanford, 40, writing for Next-Wave, an online discussion group of younger evangelicals, observes that baby-boomer churches tend to rely heavily on highly structured programs, but Xer-led churches put more emphasis on relationships. He says that boomer churches emphasize "excellence" in often profession- alized church ministries but Xer churches emphasize "realness."

Younger evangelical leaders also do not limit their outreach to particular age groups, as Mr. Webber points out: "Younger evangelicals desire to be around their parents and grandparents, and their dislike of being separated into their own group runs counter to the advice given by church-growth movements that the way to start a church is to target generations."

Boomers and Xers may use the same words differently. Baby boomers who hear the word community often think in terms of programs, such as small-group ministries, which may mean a group of 10 or so random people who don't know each other— meeting once a week, maybe, to sojourn through life together in two hours or less.

But for young evangelicals the word community reflects the need for deeper relationships. Many say that churches can't put random people together and expect honesty and transparency. Small groups are organic, emerging from relationships among people who spend time together—almost like "family." "We are filling in a deficiency," Mr. Burmeister says. "The church has an opportunity to become a family to the family-less."

A New Style of Worship

The worship style of many younger evangelicals is also different than the show-time emphasis of professional-style choirs and instrumentalism at some churches. Aaron Niequist, 27, worship director at Mars Hill, says that what people "cry out for is honesty." People want to know "how I can be really broken and not have to get cleaned up in order to sing to God."

Young people learn best from a person who is honest about his struggles.

That might even involve singing a few old-time hymns. At Doxa in Seattle traditional hymns are used, even if the music is tweaked a bit for Gen-Xers. Advent was a "big deal" that invoked the ancient church and the congregation as well, says Mr. Clem. During last year's Advent, Doxa "used traditional Scripture readings from Old Testament, Gospel and Epistles, sang hymns and carols, and lit advent candles. There was even communion."

The biggest emphasis is on Bible teaching applied to real-life situations. The preaching and teaching of Gen-Xers in these churches is far from watered down or seeker sensitive. "We know the message of self-esteem is bankrupt," says Shaun Garman, 34, pastor of Red Sea Church in Portland, Oregon. "We know we are not the center of the universe." Rather than seeing a desire for feel-good messages, he sees people who are hungry "for someone to tell them the most subversively true message—how bad they are and how great God is."

Longing for a place to come alive typifies the quest for a new way of ministry for this generation. Steve Mayer's journey landed him an internship at a small evangelistic church. His immersion into the Christianity of "evangelism only" prompted him to lead a team to Alaska to share the gospel with villagers. That trip forever changed his passion for ministry.

Among Native Americans, he saw the effects of alcoholism, suicide, depression, hopelessness, poverty, and broken families. Mr. Mayer realized that he had no answers for these situations. He had a programmed evangelistic method, but this was of little help in dealing with the situations before his eyes. "We thought we could just come in a week and change their lives" with things like VBS and other evangelistic programs, says Mr. Mayer.

So he broke all the rules of the program. He stayed out very late at night talking to people on the street, often alone, and often in co-ed contexts. He could not escape the feeling that he was selling prepackaged Christianity—and he balked. The programmed Christianity he was taught was not in touch with the brokenness of the Native Americans he met.

Of the greatest importance in the new style of worship is the application of Bible teaching to real-life situations.

For help, Mr. Mayer turned to the writings of Martin Luther King, Jr. From King he learned that Christianity should be passionate about souls and passionate about the "slums those souls reside in." Caring about souls and the real-life situations in which those souls move became authentic evangelism for Mr. Mayer. But where could he do that?

After being told by a seminary professor that many programmed-based churches wouldn't support his passion for addressing social issues, he left the world of "evangelism only" for Mars Hill. There he says he found a place where people cared about souls and life situations. "If you programmatically implement what it means to follow Jesus, you're missing it," says Mr. Mayer.

As an emerging leader at Mars Hill, Mr. Mayer recently accepted a part-time staff position in the Global Outreach office. In addition to his church work, Mr. Mayer leads a group of young adults studying justice issues and a men's group where, he says, "authenticity is simply a requirement." Mr. Mayer's passion for people and their various circumstances convinced him that in the end "you just can't think programmatically about this stuff."

It may be too early to make a sweeping generalization about where this movement is headed, but some may rightly ask: Are the concerns of the Gen-X leaders like these just a reaction? That is, in 20 years, when the children of younger evangelicals come of age and break away to start the next "new" movement, will they see the work of their parents as a healing force? Or will there be fresh brokenness to lament?

Notes

1. Anthony B. Bradley, *The Younger Evangelicals: Facing the Challenges of the New World* (Grand Rapids, MI: Baker Books, 2002), n.p.
2. The remainder of this chapter is taken from Anthony Bradley, "Keeping It Real: Younger Pastors Seek Innovative Church Settings," *World Magazine*, v. 19, n. 14, April 10, 2004 (subheadings have been added for clarity). Reprinted with permission.

CHAPTER 9

LEARNING
TO LEAD

Those who lead others are the servants of those they lead. But how do leaders know how best to serve their followers? First, compassionate leaders must know *where* they are going, for *what* purpose they are going and *how* they are going to get there. Second, they must have decided *whom* they will follow. To change Bob Dylan's lyrics just a bit, "You've got to follow somebody." Our Lord Jesus Christ, the King of kings, served God the Father. "I can of Myself do nothing," Jesus said (John 5:30); and even God the Father does not operate independently of the other two members of the Godhead. Though He is the fountainhead of the Holy Trinity, the Father always functions together with God the Son and God the Holy Spirit.

For us human beings, we either follow Christ in His church or the devil and his servants. It is granted to none of us to function alone. Of necessity, then, we cannot simply appear on the scene at 8 A.M. some bright Monday morning and say offhandedly, "Let's go, people. Follow me."

The administrator is not a slave owner but, in a real sense, the servant. In order to lead, one must serve. And not until he or she has learned how to serve and follow others can he or she become an effective leader. It was so with the Lord Jesus. With Saint Peter. With the apostle Paul. It is true with all who serve. If they lead, they serve in the fullest sense of the word.

And leadership takes time. It also takes commitment. If the job, the project, the church, the organization is to get moving and stay moving toward its stated goals, the individual at the top must always be moving out in front, setting the pace for service as he or she leads the followers.

The Best Leaders Are Led

Put another way, the driver is also the driven. He or she is driven to lead and driven to be adequate in knowledge. The leader is driven to be ahead of the followers. Then he or she is driven to stay out in front and continue to say, "Follow me."

The apostle Paul was a leader, and a highly energized organizer. Yet in his introduction to the book of Romans he speaks of himself in the third person: "From Paul, a *bond servant* of Jesus Christ, the Messiah" (1:1, *AMP*, emphasis added). And while he said, "Follow my example, as I follow the example of Christ" (1 Cor. 11:1), he also confessed in Corinth, "I came to you in weakness and fear, and with much trembling" (1 Cor. 2:3). The Greek word translated "servant" is *doulos*, literally, "slave." Peter begins his second epistle with the same introduction: "Simon Peter, a servant [doulos] . . . of Jesus Christ" (2 Pet. 1:1).

These great men were leaders, administrators, out-front men, yet they served. And Jesus, the greatest leader and follower of all, speaking of leadership to His followers, said, "Let . . . him who is the chief and leader [become] as one who serves" (Luke 22:26, *AMP*). Thus the importance of the term "servant leader."

Implicitly, Jesus is saying that leadership in its very essence is serving. It cannot be otherwise. To lead is to serve. And to serve is to become the servant of those whom one is leading. Leading is not a casual responsibility. Again, it is only when I am applying myself to the utmost that I can say before God, as did the apostle Paul, "Follow my example," and then the vital words, "as I follow Christ's!" (1 Cor. 11:1, *TLB*). It is when I have done my homework, when I have studied to show myself approved, "a [worker] who does not need to be ashamed" (2 Tim. 2:15), *then* and only then am I ready to lead and to serve.

> **Jesus is saying that leadership in its very essence is serving.**

Do you see how clearly and pragmatically service helps tie together the charismatic and official elements of leadership? If a service-oriented attitude is taken by the leader, problems are kept minimal. But if the leader seeks to lord his or her authority over the flock, trouble will always result.

The Inevitability of Inconvenience

It isn't always easy or convenient to serve people. We have things we want to do, yet as the leaders, we are responsible to be available at all times to serve those whom we lead.

Work your way through the Gospels and meditate upon the way Jesus handled interruptions. You might consider doing the same. He was often involved in meeting the need of one person when another broke in and demanded that He also speak to that need. In every case, He paused to heal, comfort or do whatever was needed, and then He proceeded with His original objective. Never did He rebuke someone with, "Can't you see that I'm busy?"

It is important to recognize that often what we consider to be interruptions are really occasions for God to break through our routines and get to us—or to enable us to minister to someone's need we may have known nothing about otherwise. Interruptions often become opportunities!

For Jesus, serving also involved ministering to people who were not always easy to deal with. In His case, there were even lepers to be ministered to. We might not be called upon to minister to "untouchables," but we might be invited to minister in a situation that is repugnant to us. Perhaps the personalities involved are abrasive or abusive, and we would much rather have suggested that they go elsewhere to settle their disputes. In each case, we, as representatives of our compassionate Lord, must appropriate the grace of God and answer the call to serve.

John Drakeford's excellent book *The Awesome Power of the Listening Ear* identifies the importance of hearing another person—

objectively and without prejudging.[1] We have learned that it is not easy. Giving careful attention to what others are saying and not seeking to give glib answers or suggestions before the other individual is completely heard are such important means of ministering. And so we must learn how to listen. It is a lesson that every servant leader must learn—repeatedly.

The Role of Reassurance

Servant leadership involves offering reassurances. An excellent example of this in Jesus' ministry has to do with a man by the name of Jairus, who was one of the rulers of the local synagogue. He approached Jesus in a distraught state. He fell at Jesus' feet and said, "My little daughter is dying. Please come and put your hands on her so that she will be healed and live" (Mark 5:23). So Jesus went with him (see v. 24).

No doubt Jairus was immediately relieved because he knew that Jesus went about healing the sick. But Jesus was suddenly stopped on the way by a woman who needed healing herself. This woman had had an issue of blood for many years. She came up behind Jesus in the crowd "and touched his cloak, because she thought, 'If I just touch his clothes, I will be healed.' Immediately her bleeding stopped" (vv. 27-29).

Jesus stopped and looked around. He asked who had touched Him. A dialogue ensued with His disciples, and then with the woman herself (see vv. 31-34). All of this took time. Meanwhile, Jairus must have despairingly wished they would all go away and let Jesus proceed to his home.

While Jesus was still ministering to the woman, some men came to Jairus from his house and told him his daughter had just died. But before Jairus could even respond to them, Jesus turned to him and offered those wonderful words of reassurance, "Don't be afraid; just believe" (v. 35). Subsequently they reached Jairus's home, and Jesus ministered life to the little girl.

Jesus' words of reassurance strengthened and comforted Jairus along that seemingly endless walk to his home. As administrators and compassionate leaders, our words of comfort and reassurance to troubled members of our flocks often enable them to continue during difficult times in their lives.

In the same way, our colleagues will be led to say just the right words to us in times of distress or difficult decision making. They perhaps do not know they are ministering to us, but God uses their words of encouragement at just the right time to bring strength in difficult circumstances. As servant leaders, we can trust Him to do that with each of us as we speak that word of affirmation when we may not be aware of the burden being carried by an employee or peer.

Reach Out and Touch Someone

While serving will sometimes require physically acknowledging others, not all of us are comfortable with touching others. Jesus ministered to people in different ways. Some He touched; others He merely spoke to. He was sensitive to the Father's will for people's differing needs. And He met each person's need right where that person was. Recall the woman with the issue of blood, the demon-possessed man, the blind man at the pool—and so many others.

Sometimes a physical touch is the only salve that will provide healing. As the Holy Spirit directs, provide that physical touch. A warm hand on the arm with an encouraging word can be of enormous help for the recipient.

Serving doesn't come easily to everyone. Some don't always like to serve continually; and when they do, they often want to choose whom they serve. But those who lead are called equally to serve. The two cannot be separated.

With this in mind, many will have to rethink their concept of serving. If you carry a negative view of servanthood, or if you believe that the idea of service connotes the idea of being "not as good as" another person, you will tend to resent your service to others. This means you will have to accept serving as part of leadership by an act of the will. Then, through a further act of the will, you will have to choose to serve with joy.

Fast Track to Learning Servant Leadership

The following three suggestions are given to help people eager to serve:

1. *Institute plans in your life that are conducive to serving.* It is easy to think of yourself as the one who gives the orders and calls the shots and to hold yourself aloof from the troops. Such an attitude might work for a time, but it will soon lead to organizational break down. Authority must always move hand-in-hand with service, because the troops need a leader who leads by example—not from a distance and by directive only.

To know what's going on in your organization, do a walk through. Frequently set aside a couple of hours on a regular basis to see what's going on. Step into offices. Ask people about needs and special accomplishments and joys. Discuss briefly means and methods of meeting needs. Often, a matter can be handled on the spot with a simple "word in season" (Prov. 15:23). All it takes is a little thoughtfulness.

Authority must always move hand-in-hand with service.

2. *Begin patterning your serving after that of Jesus.* After all, our Lord is the ultimate Servant. Study His means and methods of serving. Notice His manner of speaking,

His compassionate expressions, His availability.

3. *Take periodic self-inventory.* The following exercise will be useful in helping you look at service in a new light and to get a handle on where you are in a serving frame of reference. If you complete the six brief items, you will begin to see yourself somewhat more objectively in the matter of serving. Rate yourself on each question with a score from 1 to 10, with 1 being low and 10 being high.

- Am I secure enough within myself and in my relationship to Christ to be able to serve others in positive ways without threatening my own self-worth?
- Am I truly committed to serving those whom I lead, to actualize their potential?
- Am I willing to face the new demands and new disciplines that serving will impose on me?
- Am I willing to make decisive acts of self-relinquishing each day, which is the price often required of those who serve?
- Am I willing to take the place of a learner in general, and a listener in particular, to establish and strengthen relationships between myself and the people I serve?
- Am I willing to accept as God's purpose that the central meaning of my life is serving?

In light of the score you give yourself, ask, "Do I consider myself to be one committed to serving?" If the score is lower than 5, ask, "What is blocking or hindering my desire to serve?"

A final question that might enable you to better evaluate yourself and improve your score is, "What definite, precise action should I take in order to serve in a more Christlike manner?"

And then act upon the answer!

If you are to follow Jesus—and, if like the apostle Paul, that is your stated aim—then you will become a compassionate leader—one who cares enough to serve.

Note

1. John Drakeford, *The Awesome Power of the Listening Ear* (Waco, TX: Word Books, 1967).

THE **ULTIMATE** JOY

Servant leadership is not easily mastered. It doesn't come naturally to sinners saved by the grace of God. But when learned and practiced, it gives divine truth a luster and makes wisdom smile. Of course, not everyone is called to be a compassionate servant leader, only to have a servant's heart. Each servant leader has a special, divine calling.

Consider Nehemiah. This Jew, devoted completely to Jehovah, was able to persuade Artaxerxes of Persia to release him from captivity so that he could return to Jerusalem and rebuild the Temple that had been destroyed by Israel's enemies (see Neh. 2:1-9). This was not a project for the faint-hearted. In Jerusalem, Nehemiah "purged out the foreigners, and assigned tasks to the priests and Levites, making certain that each knew his work" (Neh. 13:30). These stalwart individuals soon restored sacrifices and offerings in the Jews' temple at Jerusalem because their leader, Nehemiah, was a true servant leader who lived to bring glory to God and to His people.

Applying the Principles of God's Word

Like any worthwhile discipline of life, change comes slowly as we submit to the authority of our Lord Jesus Christ moment by moment, and as we apply the following principles of God's Word to our daily lives:

1. *Mastering the principles of servant leadership is essential if we are to fulfill our role.* Every believer is called to be a servant of Jesus Christ and to serve others in His name. The Chief Shepherd is the silent witness to every act, the unseen Guide on every path. He longs to help us and encourage us by His power and love. All leadership by Christians should be carried out with humility, patience and dependence upon the One who set for us an

example so that we can follow in His steps.

2. *Servant leadership begins with our attitude.* As Jesus Christ took upon Himself the very nature of a servant, so we are admonished to live. This is not natural to anyone. Only as we surrender to Christ can we become servant leaders. Only as we are led into desert experiences can His attitude become ours. If we are to lead as servants, our hearts must be filled and controlled by the person of the Holy Spirit. Servant leadership begins with our attitude.

3. *Love is essential for servant leadership.* Central to the authentic lifestyle of a servant leader is a heart full of love for God and others. Then this love must be translated into a leadership style and activity. It's the meaning of the apostle John's admonition: "Dear children, let us not love with words of the tongue, but with actions and in truth" (1 John 3:18). This active love of Jesus Christ is accompanied by all the fruit of the Spirit, including joy, peace and patience. A leader possessed with those attractive qualities is not difficult to follow. He or she uses the power of leadership to lovingly build up the lives of those who follow—not for personal gain or the fulfillment of ego. Compassionate leaders are servant leaders. They are lovers, givers and builders.

Compassionate leaders are lovers, givers and builders.

4. *Biblical models teach us how to be servant leaders.* It is part of the character of God not merely to tell believers what to do but also how to do it. Then, of course, He gives us the power of the Holy Spirit to enable us to do it.

God also gives us role models to show us what servant leadership is all about. Although they are not perfect, they point the way toward the practice of authentic servant leadership. Our Lord invites us to live as He lived, to minister as He ministered and to lead as He led—in a spirit of compassion and service.

5. *The role of the good shepherd illustrates servant leadership.* Jesus uses the example of a good shepherd to help us understand the qualities and practices of an effective servant leader. The figure is used extensively in both the Old and New Testaments. A good shepherd (a) knows his or her sheep; (b) is willing to lay down his or her life for the sheep; and (c) leads the sheep. As servant leaders, we know the people entrusted to our care, and we are willing to be inconvenienced—even to lay down our lives for the people we lead, helping them to do the will of God.

6. *Servant leaders must also know how to be servant followers.* Nobody is exclusively a servant leader. Obedience is the key to Christian discipleship. Active obedience is what Christian discipleship is all about. God asks us to obey Him and the leaders He has entrusted to us. The Scriptures ask us to submit to the authority of our leaders—even kings and rulers (see 1 Pet. 2:13). We should allow leadership to be a joy to them. If we want to be effective servant leaders, we must first be effective servant followers.

7. *Servant leaders are accountable to God.* Servant leadership is not only a privilege, but it is also a responsibility. The apostle James warns that we will be judged by God with greater strictness than others who are only followers (see Jas. 3:1). Peter declares that the Chief Shepherd, Jesus Christ, will someday reward us according to our track record. There is no such thing as servant leadership within the kingdom of God that lacks accountability. Therefore, we should be careful to follow the Lord with all of our hearts and minds and strength. And we should invite others to follow us only as closely as we are following our Lord Jesus Christ.

8. *Servant leaders must lead by choice.* Our Lord desires that our servant leadership go far beyond a quality of leadership that merely responds to a legal responsibility or to a spiritual duty. God wants us to lead willingly and eagerly. The highest calling

of a servant leader is to serve God and then to serve the people entrusted to His care. Every servant leader is tempted to be motivated by pride. Instead, God helps us to become humble—like Jesus—and to lead with kindness and gentleness.

With Obedience Comes Blessing

Our ongoing temptation is to critique others, to write a checklist of the shortcomings of the leaders in our lives. Who could pass the test? Not our parents, not our pastors, not our employers—not any number of other significant leaders who touch our lives.

Instead of measuring others, compare these principles of servant leadership with your own style of leadership—not to condemn or to pass judgment, but to help you identify areas that need improvement. The purpose of this book is to encourage you and to enable you to take positive steps toward becoming an effective servant leader.

You are not alone in this worthy pursuit. Other Christian brothers and sisters are standing with you. Find a group of people in your church or community who would like to become effective servant leaders.

Then rest assured that our Lord is ready to help each pilgrim who searches for opportunities to act as a servant leader. He wants to empower you and to encourage you as you follow Jesus as Lord and submit to the control of the Holy Spirit.

There is no end of possibilities for developing compassionate leadership.

There is no end of possibilities for developing compassionate leadership. Tomorrow, new opportunities will present themselves. How will you meet them? What difference can you make?

Moses might have asked the same question. He resisted the temptation to remain in the luxury of Pharaoh's court and became

God's servant leader to deliver the people of God from bondage. David, a mighty man of valor, wrote psalms and played the harp. Solomon became the wisest man who ever lived, and Joshua led Israel's armies into battle.

But there are more recent examples that authenticate God's truth for those in need: the deed of kindness you did for a new family on your street; your gesture of friendship toward a lonely soul; your word of witness to a lost neighbor; your gift of money to a desperate family—all were recorded by the One we have been called to serve.

Servant leadership is not natural. It requires the supernatural— the presence and power of almighty God our savior. May He help each of us lead with a servant's heart. Then both God Himself and those with whom we share our lives will be blessed.

SEASONED COUNSEL FOR **EMERGING** LEADERS

As we wrote in the introduction, discussions about leadership usually focus on power, management and organization. Add the word "servant" to modify leadership, and you have the theme of this book—leadership as our Lord intended it when He invited us to follow Him "who came not to be served, but to serve" (Mark 10:34).

Keeping It Fresh

Uppermost in the mind of a compassionate leader is the constant quest to know and understand the will of God, and to seek His wisdom and guidance. "When a person's development as a leader is finished," wrote E. A. Filene, "that leader is finished." Effective leaders must be willing to be in the state of constant learning. There is no relaxing or even plateauing. Executive leaders recognize that they are at the pinnacle of management, but they will stay there only as long as they are willing to keep listening and learning.

Servant leaders are characterized by a thorough and ever-expanding knowledge of God's Word. They put to use their biblical wisdom, and understand clearly the grace of God. They are humble, courageous and compassionate as they keep in order their priorities of God, spouse, children, family, friends, job and community.

Keeping Your Eyes on Jesus

In 1987, I (Paul) wrote a book on servant leadership. Within that book, I admitted that I was not an expert on the subject. In fact, I probably was only in kindergarten in my understanding of that important subject. I also confessed that I did not know of many role models to whom I could look who were demonstrating the biblical concept of servant leadership. However, I longed to grow in that area of my life and leadership.

Now, nearly 20 years later, the subject of servant leadership has enjoyed a virtual explosion of books, articles and even video productions. However, the model that I discovered to be the best when I was writing that book remains my model today. I highly commend Him to you.

Of course, it is Jesus. He was, and is, the ultimate servant leader. He humbled Himself, emptied Himself and became the servant. In His own words, He came to Earth not "to be served, but to serve, and to give his life as a ransom for many" (Matt. 20:28).

If we want to be effective servant leaders, we need to become more and more like Jesus. And the only way for that to happen is for us to surrender ourselves to Him more and more and to live under the control of the Holy Spirit. We need to lead "the Jesus way."

Building a Team

Let the following principles guide you as you seek to develop your own God-given abilities and get on with the Lord's work!

Servant leaders anticipate crises that could inhibit or destroy progress, and stay ahead of them. If you cannot, then take steps to weather them. Build battle-ready staffs that are composed of soldiers who trust their officers and will fight for the cause they mutually embrace.

Servant leaders develop team members into strong, tenacious workers able to withstand the difficulties, obstacles and crises that an organization can experience. These types of team members embrace the vision and purpose of the organization and believe in them.

After careful thought and prayer, servant leaders define the mission of the institution. Refine its operations at all levels. Make each explanation specific, simple, clear and focused. Encourage your team to do the right things better because they are committed to something in which they really believe. Your mission statement will identify the precise opportunity indicating the competence and commitment that is needed.

Servant leaders demonstrate in each critical choice the discipline of abandonment. A weak leader sees that something doesn't work and abandons it. Look upon each change of course not as a threat but as an opportunity to do the right thing correctly and stay on track. Systematic innovation should be an ongoing policy that releases energy for progress. Seize these opportunities. Implement innovations and organize new plans separately, lest they get bogged down in an antiquated system.

Servant leaders find and nurture other leaders who display good character. These will be believers who are enemies of mediocrity, who take their roles seriously, who think "we" rather than "I," and who know and accept that they are constantly on trial. Your job is to prepare new leaders so that you can eventually leave the organization without causing it to collapse. The people you select should be allowed to keep their personality and individuality while they build an organization that can go on without you.

Servant leaders balance long-range goals with short-term ones. This allows your colleagues to get a clear view of the big picture without disregarding the details. Your duty is to create a balance between opportunity and risk.

Servant leaders do not expect associates to catch on immediately. As a rule, people will not understand something until it is explained in many different ways and from several angles. Finally, the light will dawn!

Servant leaders work hard at finding able people to succeed staff members ready to retire. Look upon your development of people as the primary foundation on which to build. Make certain that strengths are identified so that able people surface to undertake delicate assignments. Behind everything you do should be the goal of developing servant leaders who can take over when you leave.

Servant leaders develop people as the primary foundation. The organization is secondary. When people are developed, the organization gets what it needs to function and accomplish its purpose. When you build upon what people are, change comes naturally because people are changing constantly. The realization of staff members' potential means strength for any organization. And a good servant leader "abandons" the staff (but not entirely) so that people will have the space they need to realize their potential and be accountable to achieve the desired results.

Leaders delegate when certain clear rules are followed in the development of understudies.

- Delegated tasks are clearly defined.
- Delegated tasks have mutually understood goals and accepted deadlines for progress reports and the accomplishment of the task.
- Delegated tasks or responsibilities are balanced with the right proportion of authority, yet with clear accountability for the performance and reporting of the right job carried out properly.
- Delegated tasks are wisely and appropriately entrusted to others. Leaders avoid the danger of delegating everything because an effective leader cannot delegate what is his own specific responsibility for which he has authority and for which he is accountable until it is accomplished. He may have the responsibility of being the keeper of the vision and its protector until sufficient

transvisioning has occurred (when team members understand and embrace the vision as their own) and when new leaders begin to surface.

Servant leaders' accountability is not shunned. Excellence is really a measurement that requires a standard of accountability as we pursue the process of reaching the goal, keeping the priorities in place and motivating understudies to succeed. In striving for accountability, we must never settle for the good, only for the excellent.

Servant leaders are mentors. They encourage others to be mentors as well so that the right connections between people happen without having to force the structure.

Servant leaders think through priorities. That's hard because the process always involves abandoning things that look attractive, things that people both inside and outside the organization are pushing for. But if you don't concentrate on your institution's resources, you are not going to get results. This may be the ultimate test of leadership—the ability to think through a priority decision and to make it stick.

Servant leaders convert good intentions into effective results, busyness into productivity, "routine status quo" philosophy into a philosophy of "changing to improve." Instead of resting on their laurels when the organization is successful, leaders bring more change, refocus and loudly proclaim, "Let's improve it!"

Servant leaders accept responsibility for major decision-making in the face of risk. For this reason, they take time for thought and keep away from trivial matters. They know that a decision is a commitment to *action*, not merely pious intentions.

Servant leaders seek to do the right things in the right department or organization. They ask tough questions such as, "Where do I belong as a person?" The answer to this requires an understanding of what kind of work or ministry environment is needed for understudies to do their best. When they are successful at something, they run with it! This is the most effective road to self-renewal. Don't brush success aside and stay problem-focused. Run with the part that is proving successful; match the needs and opportunities of the organization with its competence and strengths.

Servant leaders accept some dissent and disagreement as healthy when decisions need to be made concerning important matters. If there is no dissent, and there is complete consensus, then you can be sure that nobody did his or her homework! Decisions by acclamation reveal that a decision is, or was, made about the symptom rather than about the real cause.

Disagreement can really be a way of getting right answers to hard questions. It's important to discover *what* is right for the organization (since each person sees reality differently), not *who* is right (e.g., "Mr. K. must be right because his idea worked before"). If you can bring dissent and disagreement to a common understanding of what the discussion is all about, you create unity and commitment. An old saying, going back to Aristotle, became an axiom in the early Christian Church: *In essentials, unity; in action, freedom; and in all things, trust.* And trust requires that dissent come out into the open and that it be seen as honest disagreement.

Servant leaders look at performance. In the process he or she ensures that each person has a mentor to help guide him or her, a teacher to develop the person's skills, an evaluator to check progress, and an encourager to cheer the individual on (even after he stumbles or falls flat on his face).

Servant leaders know how to find, motivate and maintain committed people—people who work for a cause, not only for a living. They develop these people so that they can do better than themselves, and then they entrust the organization to these new leaders. In this way they build for tomorrow. For this reason, the servant leader must motivate a group to continue until the task is accomplished triumphantly. This involves the development and maintenance of a cohesive team that understands clearly that "united we stand, divided we fall." In all of this, it is important to be sensitive and alert to help meet each individual's needs and to allow each team member to contribute in his or her own unique way.

Servant leaders ensure that there are effective boards and executive committees for their organizations. They are constantly concerned with formulating a strategy of leadership development; selecting those with leadership potential; training leaders at every level; establishing career development policy at every level within the organization; performing research and development of new ideas, courses, training and so on; formulating an efficient, effective organizational structure; encouraging the self-development of young "leaders-to-be"; developing and maintaining a warm, friendly organizational climate; and modeling an effective managerial leadership.

Servant leaders manage change. Not to admit that there is constant change is to be blind or to capitulate to the slow death syndrome of the status quo. People must change their attitudes, skills, expectations, perceptions and behavior. The structure of the organization might need to change in the areas of authority relations, redesigning roles, jobs and responsibilities—maybe even doing away with certain functions, positions, departments or committees that have become unproductive and obsolete. Then servant leaders have to keep up constantly with changing technology that affects the way they process their work.

Servant leaders perform well when they can blend the following approaches expertly in their leadership roles:

- Power-influence approach which gives certain effectiveness in terms of the amount of power the leader has, the type of power, how it is exercised and how the leader is perceived by others
- Behavior approach which emphasizes what managerial leaders actually do on the job and in their roles
- Trait approach which emphasizes the personal attributes of leaders such as tireless energy, penetrating intuition, uncanny foresight, persuasiveness, motivation, skills and so on
- Situational approach, which emphasizes the variable factors in a given situation that will influence the direction of the person or organization

Doing It for the Least of These

In an attitude of prayer, with conscientious determination and with a clear conscience before God and your fellowman, focus your efforts as a compassionate servant leader on meeting the needs of the *task*, of the *individual* and of the *team* amid constantly changing situations and the demand for productivity. Meeting needs in these three areas and blending them together will create a cohesive, productive team that achieves a common purpose while respecting and developing each individual member.

Lay aside any temptation toward laziness. Slay the dragon of fear of failure. Deal with any lack of discipline. Determine not to buckle in the face of ridicule. Keep ever before you a sense of direction and purpose that allows understudies to recognize and grasp their gifts and abilities.

And let your obedience be to the first Compassionate Servant Leader, who reminds us that when we do anything "for the least of these," we do it for Him.

CHRISTIAN
LEADERSHIP
AND LEADERSHIP
STYLES

Leadership can be looked at from many different angles. First, leadership is a *position*. Companies have leaders; organizations have leaders; groups have leaders. Second, leadership is a *relationship*. Leaders are persons who have followers—by definition. People may follow because of inspiration, self-interest or because of organizational structures, but followers there must be. Third, leadership is about *action*. Leaders are known by the leadership acts they perform. A person may have a long list of the attributes or traits of a leader, but if he or she never takes leadership action, he or she is not a leader. *Christian* leadership differs from other forms of leadership basically in its motivation, the "why?" of its actions.[1]

How to Define a Leader

For years, there has been a running argument about how to define a leader. Is a person a leader because of the qualities or attributes brought to the role? Is one a leader as a result of a relationship to a group? Is a person a leader because of the things done?

There has been a general confusion between the person or role of the leader and that of the manager (or administrator, executive, director, general, ruler or whatever name the position carries). This confusion is quite natural. People who turn out to be good leaders find themselves in positions of leadership. Because they are seldom identified as leaders until the time they assume the leadership role, it is difficult to distinguish between the individual and the role.

In his landmark book *The Practice of Management*, Peter Drucker, the dean of management experts, wrote, "Leadership is of utmost importance. Indeed, there is no substitute for it. But leadership cannot be created or promoted. It cannot be taught or learned."[2]

Drucker believes that the task of the organization is to create the conditions under which potential leadership qualities become effective.

To put it another way, leadership qualities are part of the basic makeup of the individual. Those qualities will not necessarily become evident until that individual is found in a leadership situation. Most, if not all, of the men and women who are found in leadership positions have been put there because their leadership ability has been recognized. If you or your associates do not have the basic makeup of a leader, you will not become one. But it does not follow that men and women who are potential leaders will automatically find leadership roles.

What, then, is the definition of a leader? The most useful definition is "a person who has followers in a given situation." Not every person will be a leader in every situation. But a leader *will be identified* by the fact that he or she has followers.

Are There Basic Qualities?

Are there, then, any basic qualities that all leaders will have to some measure? Observers of leaders (and those who have been leaders themselves) seem to point to a handful of attributes that seem to be universal. Some of these attributes are either genetic or are closely wrapped up in the special environment. Others are acquired.

Selfless dedication is how General Eisenhower describes the first quality.[3] There is a quality about leaders—a belief in what they are doing, the goals they are trying to reach, the cause that they espouse—that transcends the person. Leaders are willing to sacrifice even themselves to accomplish the task.

This takes *courage*. To hold on in spite of the apparent obstacles, make a decision with inadequate information, or risk reputation and material well-being require courage based on conviction.

A major portion of this courage will demonstrate itself in *decisiveness*. Decisions must be made. Other people vacillate. The leader makes a decision and moves ahead.

Leadership requires *persuasiveness*. If men and women are to follow, they must be convinced that the goals and aspirations of the leader are worthy of their dedication and be motivated to attempt them.

Interestingly, there is almost universal agreement that the most outstanding leaders have had a *humility* that has resulted in their accepting responsibility for failure as well as success.

Up to this point we have been describing qualities that might be held by almost anyone in any walk of life. But for the vast majority of leadership situations, there must be *competence*. The individual must have skills in the area in which he or she is working. Without competence, few wars will be won, no ocean liner will dock, and no organization (Christian or other) will long survive. Competence, of course, assumes intelligence and creativity to whatever degree required.

Many people think of leaders as having a great deal of personality or charisma. Both personal observation and a small amount of research will quickly show you that "personality" is *not* one of the basic qualities. There are leaders who are personally warm and affable, those who are cold and aloof, those who are very public in their style, and those who are quiet.

Nor can leaders be typed by the way in which they go about their task. There are many different styles of leadership—dictatorial, autocratic, benevolent, democratic. Some individuals lead by example. Others lead by sensing the direction of the crowd. Some are problem solvers who work well in groups. Others may pride themselves on their quick decision-making ability. In the complex societies in which most of us work, those who hold positions of leadership in dynamic organizations have learned to adopt their style to the situation.

How to Find Good Leaders

If Drucker is right—if leadership "cannot be taught or learned"—what can we do to find, equip and select the best leaders? The answer lies in building organizations that encourage and promote these basic qualities. Leadership *is* situational. It is a combination of the right leader leading the right group in the right set of circumstances.

The most competent leader is the one who can continue to exercise leadership in the broadest number of situations. Do you want to attract and nurture good leaders? Build into your organization goals and objectives that require dedication and courage. Set high standards of conduct, responsibility and performance. Demonstrate respect for the individual and his or her work. Create a climate where good leaders will be recognized and nurtured.

Once such a climate exists, good leaders will begin to identify themselves. It is at this point that training can begin. As we said earlier, leaders must have adequate competence in their field. If an individual is to assume broader responsibilities, he or she must have the specific training needed. This can be obtained formally by more academic work or on-the-job training. If on-the-job training, then care should be taken that both the person and supervisor understand the (measurable) objectives of the training.

It does not follow that because a person is technically outstanding that he or she is necessarily a leader. Putting a technically competent person in a leadership position when he or she is not a leader may only serve to prove the Peter Principle: "Everyone eventually rises to the level of his or her incompetency."

What Is Christian Leadership?

So far, we have said very little about *Christian* leadership other than to note that it differs basically in its motivation. However, it is interesting to note that those organizations that place a high priority on the worth of the individual have high standards of personal conduct, have good communication (both up and down) and have righteous convictions outperform the others. Too often in the past, Christian organizations have had lower standards for individual and corporate performance than secular ones.

What is *Christian* leadership? It is leadership motivated by love and given over to service. It is leadership that has been subjected to the control of Christ and His example. The best Christian leaders exemplify to the utmost all those attributes of selfless dedication, courage, decisiveness, compassion and persuasiveness that mark the great leader. The truly Christian leader has discovered that leadership begins with the towel and the basin—in the role of a servant. *Selfless dedication* is possible because the Christian knows that God has a grand strategy of which he is a part. *Courage* is magnified by the power that comes through the indwelling Spirit. *Decisiveness* comes from knowing that ultimate responsibility does not lie with Him. *Persuasiveness* is based on allegiance to a cause that transcends all causes. *Humility* results from knowing that it is God who does the work.

Are you a Christian leader? Lead! The *purpose* of leadership is to lead.

Leadership Styles

What is leadership? We have just seen that no one seems to be really sure. We are able to define what *managers* do, but the clos-

est we seem to be able to come to a broadly acceptable definition of leadership is "that which leaders do." When we try to
define leader, about all the agreement we can get is that leaders
lead.

Management theorists—perhaps in despair over defining
leadership—have attempted to picture it in terms of *style*. In
using such a broad term, they are attempting to describe how
a person operates, rather than what he or she is. If you think
about a number of leaders whom you know personally, you
can probably come up with your own summation of their
style: "He's a player/coach kind of guy" or "She's a prima
donna" or "He's a one-man show." In other words, we tend to
characterize a leader on the way he or she leads by our personal perception of him or her. It follows that one person may
feel differently than another about a leader's style. "Style"
turns out to be the summation of how the leader goes about
carrying out the leadership function and how he or she is perceived by those whom he or she is attempting to lead or those
who may be observing from the sidelines.

What Leadership Styles Are There?

Because leadership style includes how a person operates within
the context of the organization, it is easiest to discuss different
kinds of style by describing the type of organization or situation
that either results from or is appropriate for a particular style.
Our concern for the moment is with those who are in positions
of leadership already, rather than those who are wondering
about their potential skills. We will discuss five leadership styles:
bureaucratic, permissive, laissez-faire, participative and autocratic. We will look at each one of these in terms of how the
leader operates *within the organization*.

- *Bureaucratic*—This is a style marked by a continual reference to organization rules and regulations. It is assumed that somehow difficulties can be ironed out if everyone will abide by the rules. Decisions are made by parliamentary procedures. The leader is a diplomat and learns how to use the majority rule as a way to get people to perform. Compromise is a way of life because in order to have one decision accepted by the majority, it is often necessary to give in on another one.

- *Permissive*—Here the desire is to keep everyone in the group satisfied. Keeping people happy is the name of the game. It is assumed that if people feel good about themselves and others, the organization will function, and thus the job will get done. Coordination often suffers with this style.

- *Laissez-faire*—This is practically no leadership at all and allows everything to run its own course. The leader simply performs a maintenance function. For example, a pastor may act as a figurehead as far as the leadership of the organization is concerned and concern himself or herself only with preaching, while others are left to work out the details of how the organization should operate. This style is sometimes used by leaders who are away a great deal or who have been temporarily put in charge.

- *Participative*—This is used by those who believe the way to motivate others is to involve them in the decision-making process. This hopefully creates goal ownership and a feeling of shared purpose. Here the problem is the delay in action during times of crisis.

- *Autocratic*—This is marked by reliance upon authority and usually assumes that people will not do anything unless told to. It discourages innovation. The leader sees himself or herself as indispensable. However, decisions can be made quickly.

What Do These Styles Assume?

Notice that each one of these styles depends to a large extent on one's view of people and what motivates them. Because the function of leadership is to lead, getting people to follow is of primary importance.

- *Bureaucratic leaders* somehow believe that everyone can agree on the best way to do things and that there is some system outside of human relationships that can be used as a guide—hence the rules and regulations.

- *Permissive leaders* want everyone (including themselves) to feel good. Internal stress is viewed as being bad for the organization (and perhaps even un-Christian).

- *Laissez-faire leaders* assume either that the organization is running so well that they can't add to it or that the organization really doesn't need a focal point of leadership.

- *Participative leaders* usually enjoy solving problems and working with others. They assume that others feel the same way; therefore, the most will be accomplished by working together and sharing all decisions and goals.

· *Autocratic leaders* assume that people will only do what
they are told to do and/or that they know what is best.
(In other words, autocratic leaders may appear to be
dictators.)

Which Style Is Best?

Leaders are different. But so are followers! This is another way
of saying that some situations demand one style of leadership,
while others demand a different one. At any given time, the
leadership needs of an organization may vary from another
time. Because organizations have difficulty continually changing their leaders, it follows that those leaders will need *different
styles* at *different times*. The appropriate style depends a great
deal on the task of the organization, the phase of life of the
organization, and the needs of the moment. Organizations
need to renew themselves, and different leadership styles are
often needed.

What might be some examples of how the *task of the organization* affects leadership style? A fire department cannot perform
without at least some autocratic leadership. When the time comes
for the organization to perform—to do what it was designed to
do—autocratic leadership is a must. There is no time to sit down
and discuss how to attack the fire. One trained person has to
decide for the group, and the group must abide by the decision.
Later on there may be a more free discussion on which way will be
best next time. On the other hand, a medical group might best be
operated with a permissive style.

An autocratic style may even be needed in a Christian organization! In times of crisis, such as the evacuation of mission

personnel, or the need to radically reduce costs, the leader often must act unilaterally.

Organizations go through different *phases in their life*. During periods of rapid growth and expansion, autocratic leadership may work very well. For example, the founder of a new Christian organization, or the founding pastor of a church, is often a charismatic figure who knows intuitively what is to be done and how to do it. Because the vision is his or hers, he or she is best able to impart it to others without discussion. But during periods of slow growth or consolidation, the organization needs to be much more reflective to attempt to be more efficient. Participative leadership may be the order of the day.

Both of these considerations need to be tempered by the *needs of the moment*. Using autocratic leadership may work well for fire fighting (either real or figurative), but it will probably be less than successful in dealing with a personal problem. An emergency in the medical group may demand that someone assume (autocratic) leadership.

Fitting Style to Organization

It follows that ideally a leader should have many different styles. He or she should be a person for all seasons, shifting from the permissiveness of summer to the demands of winter.

Looking at it from the side of the organization, the organization needs to adopt a *strategy for effectiveness,* taking into account its needs and its "product." Most voluntary organizations and not-for-profit organizations are founded on the assumption of a common vision and shared goals. They have a strategy of *seeking success* (reaching their goals). When the organization is young, the founder can depend on his or her strength of vision to attract others who share his or her goals. However, as the organization becomes successful, other means of maintaining a common vision will be needed. If the leadership style is not modified to include participative sharing of goals, too often the organization will adopt the strategy of *avoiding failure*. When the organization reaches a size at which an autocratic style will no longer work if the leader is unable to switch to a participative style, many times he or she is forced (perhaps unknowingly) to adopt a laissez-faire style. Meanwhile the second level of leadership (which is now forced to run the organization) is most likely to adopt a bureaucratic style.

Where Do You Go from Here?

What is your leadership style? A cursory examination of some of the management literature will help you discover it. Hopefully, you will discover that you have exercised different types of leadership style at different times. Do you have evidence that you *can* change your style as needed? Or, as you think of the decisions that have been made in the past six months, do you discover that they were always made the same way (by you, by others, together, or by the bureaucracy)?

What kind of leadership does your organization need at this time? What is its task? What phase of organizational growth are you in? What are the different needs of this moment? Analyze this with help from your board and leadership team members. Are different styles of leadership needed for different areas of organizational life?

Review your calendar of meetings for the past two weeks. What happened in those meetings? Did you go to the meeting just to announce your own decision (autocratic style)? Did you go to meetings expecting to work with the group to arrive at a decision (participative style)? Did you go expecting to sit back and let others worry about the problem (permissive style)? Or, did you go intending to use the parliamentary procedure to make sure that the ship stayed on an even keel (bureaucratic style)? Perhaps you didn't go at all (laissez-faire)!

If you discovered that you handled each meeting in the same way, you are probably locked into one style and should consider modifying your style as a function of the situation that you are in. By deciding before the meeting the style you will adopt, you will give yourself the advantage of being able to observe the response of the other members of the meeting. If you have been limiting yourself to one style, sudden changes will often result in confusion to others. It may be necessary for you to very clearly spell out the ground rules as to how you are anticipating the decision-making process will work.

Notes
1. The information contained in this appendix was adapted from Ted W. Engstrom and Edward R. Dayton, *The Art of Management for Christian Leaders* (Grand Rapids, MI: Zondervan Publishing House, 1989), pp. 23-35.
2. Peter Drucker, *The Practice of Management* (New York: Harper and Row, 1954), p. 158.
3. Dwight David Eisenhower, "What is Leadership," *Reader's Digest,* June 1965, p. 50.

MAKING YOUR BOSS
SUCCESSFUL

D o you work for an individual or for an organization? Do your subordinates work for you or for your church or agency? Or do they perhaps think they work just for the Lord?[1]

A primary task of each person in his or her organization is to make his or her boss successful. If you assumed that you went to work for an organization and still work for one, this may seem strange. But the most effective organizations are those that see themselves as the sum total of their members. Once a person joins an organization, effectiveness in the organization is dependent on how he or she relates to superiors, peers and subordinates.

Relationships are a foundation for an effective organization. The relationship between a superior and subordinate is very much like the relationship between the biblical model of the body. The hand needs the wrist. The hand cannot say, "I work for the *body,* and therefore, I have no need of the wrist!"

Organizations Are the Result of People

If two people agree to saw a log in half, an organization has been formed. Agreement on a common purpose is assumed. How well they perform or do not perform their task is completely dependent on how they work together.

If they decide to go into partnership, a more permanent organization has been formed, but its effectiveness will continue to depend on their relationship to each other. Their common purpose remains: cut logs in as efficient a manner as possible.

But perhaps they decide to expand. They subcontract work to other teams. Now the relationship becomes more subtle. However, performance is still easily measurable. The second team's value to the budding company is directly related to how many cut logs they produce.

But let us go further. Success continues to follow their efforts. A sawmill is erected, and then eventually a lumberyard. Twenty years later there are more than 500 employees, including 50 who manage a large tree farm, 47 who work in 3 lumberyards, a 10-person sales force, and 115 people in a sash-and-door division. "Cutting logs" has now become "supplying finished lumber, sash and doors to the home-building industry." What began as a highly relational enterprise has now become diffused. One can now go to work for the tree division of Jones Brothers Inc., or for the sawmill or the sales force. Roles are identified: "I am a millhand." "I am a saleswoman." "I am a manager." Roles and organization become more significant than relationships. Whereas it was rather simple to identify the contribution of the man at the other end of a bucksaw, the contribution of the millwright who keeps all the machines in order is much more difficult to measure.

Nevertheless, regardless of how the employees think of themselves, the organization is made up of its *people,* and without them it dies.

Organizations Tend Toward Bureaucracy

Just as success is often the result of effectiveness, so success tends to breed efficiency (not necessarily the same thing!) Job descriptions are written (good). Procedures are defined (good). Policies are formalized (good). People become more interested in efficiency than effectiveness (bad). As the distance in time and space increases between those who make management decisions and those who carry them out, it becomes more and more difficult for individuals to feel as though they are an integral part of the whole—to believe that they "count." The day comes when the millhand no longer believes that what he does is important. The millwright gets sloppy in oiling the machines. Managers become more interested in their prerogatives than performance, and the organization starts to slide.

Some Assumptions About Organizations

What assumptions are inherent in this scenario?

- Organizations are the result of structural relationships between people.
- Organizations succeed or fail on the strength of these relationships.
- The relationships should be based on assumed common goals, personal motivation, and an ability (skill) to carry out the task (role).

Not so obvious in our narrative was the assumption that the organization has developed standards of both personal and organizational ethics.

Assumptions of the Individual

When individuals join the organization, they also have some assumptions. They assume:

- The organization can use their abilities.
- They will "get along" with their fellow employees.
- The organization has certain ethical and moral standards and norms (rules) that will be maintained.

A failure of the organization, or the individual, to live up to any of these assumptions usually leads to a failure of the individual and ultimately to separation.

Fitting In to the Organization

We often describe people as "fitting in," either very well or not so well. What makes a person fit in? There are obviously many factors: skill, personality, experience. But a great deal depends on whether that person sees himself or herself as relating to an organization or an individual. We join organizations. We work for and with people.

Making a Success Out of Your Boss

Interpreting and acting on what your superior wants and needs, rather than what you believe the organization wants and needs, has some very practical and important consequences. First, it keeps the lines of responsibility clear. Second, it makes communication much simpler. Third, it keeps loyalties from becoming divided. The result is a much more effective organization and much happier staff members.

Our immediate response to the idea of "my boss first, my organization next" might be, "What if he (or she) is a bum? What if he (or she) is acting unethically?" That's easy. Get a new boss! How? Leave the organization, if you have to. But if it is not a question of ethics, do everything you can to make him (or her) effective.

So how do you make your boss a success? Here are some practical ideas.

- *Represent your boss fairly.* Your boss is human and is bound to have weaknesses and shortcomings. Talk about your boss's abilities and try not to discuss his or her weaknesses.

- *Try to understand your boss.* What's your boss's style? People are different. How does your boss think? *Why* does he or she think that way? What does he or she do best? Is your boss a decision maker, a problem solver, or both?

- *Try to do it your boss's way,* even if your way seems better. One day, your boss will discover your way.

- *Keep you boss informed.* Don't surprise your boss. Tell your boss about decisions you want him or her to make, what problems you anticipate, and what you plan to do.

- *Give your boss alternatives.* If you are asking for a decision, give your boss several alternatives to choose from. Think through acceptable alternatives. You'll be less disappointed, and so will he or she.

What About Company Loyalty?

Haven't military organizations like the Marines done a good job of building *esprit de corps* through "loyalty to the outfit"? What about pride in the organization?

There is little doubt that some organizations have evolved a high degree of pride in their present and past accomplishments and/or methods of operations. But such pride is especially the result of teamwork, and it becomes a spur toward greater cross-commitment rather than a detriment to it.

What About Volunteer Organizations?

Does this apply to the local church? We believe that it does. Too often the local church organization (committee, board, commission) is wrapped up in what it does rather than its goals. Volunteers may not describe the group leader in the same terms as their supervisors at work, but their concern for them should be even greater.

Does This Leave Any Room for Criticism?

Personal commitment is a three-way street: up, down, sideways. When we treat others as persons of worth, they usually respond in kind. This in turn produces a climate within which constructive change can take place.

Been working for the organization? Try working for your boss. You may like it.

Note

1. The information contained in this appendix was adapted from Ted W. Engstrom and Edward R. Dayton, *The Art of Management for Christian Leaders* (Grand Rapids, MI: Zondervan Publishing House, 1989), pp. 117-122.

LOVE IS ESSENTIAL
IN LEADERSHIP

A new commandment I give you; Love one another.
As I have loved you, so you must love one another.
All men will know that you are my disciples
if you love one another.

JOHN 13:34-35

God does not give us power to be used for our own ends or desires. His power is entrusted to us so that we are motivated to serve God and others with the love of Jesus Christ and the power of the Holy Spirit![1]

Tragically, this teaching has been ignored throughout much of Church history by a male preference for a part of Paul's teaching in Ephesians that states that wives should submit to their husbands (see Eph. 5:22). Unfortunately, the focus on service has often been downplayed along with Paul's insistence that there should be a mutual submission in love to one another out of reverence for Christ (see v. 21).

I believe that both teachings are vitally important if we are to understand the biblical concept of love in marriage and in servant leadership. When we love one another as Christ has loved us, we will submit to one another in love and we will give ourselves to one another just as Christ has done for us!

Because the word "love" is used and misused so frequently in our modern society, I think it is important for us to be certain of what it means here. The writer of 1 John gives us a simple yet profound definition when he writes, "God is love" (1 John 4:16). And from the teaching of Jesus, we learn that God's love is unconditional—we can't earn that kind of love (we don't even deserve it!).

However, the Bible gives us some additional insights for defining love in very practical, measurable terms. If we are to be servant leaders who have love as our basic motive, just how do we translate that into our day-to-day actions? After all, it is one thing to say that we should act as Christ would act, love as He loved, submit as He submitted, and serve as He served. But it is quite another thing to follow through and live out those noble words in a practical, hands-on manner.

Leading with Love

I believe an exciting model for leading with love is found in Paul's marvelous teaching in 2 Corinthians 13. In this passage, we find a graphic picture of how love is to look and behave in all of life—and especially in servant leadership. In fact, it is not inappropriate for our purposes here to substitute the words "servant leader" whenever the word "love" or "charity" is found in 2 Corinthians 13. As we do, we will discover a practical and workable definition of servant leadership. Let me show you what I mean with the following paraphrase of verses 4 through 7:

> A servant leader is patient and kind. A servant leader doesn't envy others or boast. A servant leader is not proud or rude, does not insist on having his or her own way. A servant leader does not become easily angered, doesn't hold grudges or keep a list of people's past mistakes. A servant leader is never happy with any form of evil but is always searching for truth. A servant leader always protects others, trusts others, and always hopes for the best! A servant leader never gives up.

This is a vivid description of the life of the ultimate servant leader—Jesus Christ. And this description provides a measurable model for each of us who want to be servant leaders. To be sure, if we were expected by God to pull off this kind of leadership style in our own strength, we would be destined to fail. To love and lead and serve as Jesus did requires the strength and power of Christ Himself! We can't do it without Him. However, as the apostle Paul reminds us, "I can do everything through him who gives me strength" (Phil. 4:13).

But the good news of the gospel is that we can be servant leaders! We can love as Christ loves. We can be what God wants us to be and do what God wants us to do—with His enabling power through the Holy Spirit. That is God's promise to each one of us. Paul shared this promise with young Timothy when he wrote, "For God did not give us a spirit of timidity, but a spirit of power, of love and of self-discipline" (2 Tim. 1:7).

Interestingly, the love of God and the power of God go together. Or perhaps a better way to express it is that they come together. Both are readily available to us. As Jesus prepared to conclude His earthly ministry, He took His disciples out to the Mount of Olives and gave them this promise: "You will receive power when the Holy Spirit comes on you" (Acts 1:8).

Luke's narrative in the Acts of the Apostles reveals to us that those were not only our Lord's words of commissioning, but they were also prophetic words soon to be fulfilled. In the second chapter of Acts, we read about those awesome events that took place as the Holy Spirit came to dwell within the disciples. The Spirit's power broke through their lives in remarkable ways, including the message of Peter delivered on the streets of Jerusalem when several thousands received salvation through the risen Lord (see Acts 2:38).

Before those startling events on the Day of Pentecost, there wasn't any particular evidence that Peter had much spiritual power. It is true, of course, that he had come to love Jesus during their time together. And Jesus had put a lot of trust in Peter, even to the point of calling him "the rock." The Lord said that He was going to build His church upon Peter and his leadership.

But on the night Jesus was arrested and faced His greatest trial, Peter let Jesus down. It is true that Peter was ready in the Garden of Gethsemane to protect Jesus with his sword. Peter wanted to do the right thing, but he didn't have the power to stand firm, and so he denied his Lord. He caved in and said that he didn't even know Jesus!

Many of us can identify with Peter. We are sincere and try to do our best, but that isn't good enough. After all, Peter was sincere, but he didn't have spiritual power until he received the Holy Spirit. It was then he moved out boldly to witness for Christ as a servant leader.

Russ Reid, in an excellent article entitled "What Ruins Christian Leaders? A Plan for Leashing Top Dogs," warns about the abuse of power. He quotes a famous senator who said:

> When I leave my office to go to the Senate floor, an elevator comes immediately . . . reversing direction if necessary and bypassing the floors of the other bewildered passengers aboard, in order to get me to the basement. As I walk down the corridor, a policeman notices me coming and rings for a subway car to wait for my arrival and take me to the Capitol building . . . At the Capitol, another elevator marked "For Senators Only" takes me to the Senate floor.[2]

The words belong to U.S. Senator Mark Hatfield. They are words about power—about the rights and privileges bestowed on one who has placed himself into the rarified air of Washington politics—where raw power is enshrined and seniority amply rewarded. Senator Hatfield has come to terms with his power, but he himself admits that the struggle not to abuse it never ends. Unfortunately, this arena is also filled with the stories of Christian leaders who have built tremendous ministries but who don't know how to exercise the power their creation has given them. Their early vision—with its absolute dependence on God—often has shifted to a nightmarish one-man show. "Unilateral 'seat-of-the-pants' decisions upstage good counsel. 'The Lord told me to do it' often becomes a pious platitude to justify leapfrogging over the wisdom of boards and committees."[3]

God does not give us power to be used for our own ends or desires. His power is entrusted to us so that we are motivated to serve God and others with the love of Jesus Christ and the power of the Holy Spirit! Bob Toms, who is a prominent Los Angeles attorney, shared the following insights about power and servant leadership:

> Jesus was very candid about his power and how to be great in the kingdom. "Whosoever will be chief among you, let him be your servant." Sun Szu and Niccolo Machiavelli notwithstanding, Jesus taught an inverted pyramid of power; to be a Christian leader one must (1) humble oneself, (2) submit to God's authority, and (3) serve those who need a shepherd. Leaders were to function from the bottom, not the top. Again, the Good News is absolute dynamite: political power, wealth, birth, race and sex are not prerequisites to this kind of power, and leadership and the competition for it is not keen, but a large group can be led from the bottom by the authentic Christian servant leader. Most of all, by few words and consistent deeds an eternally eloquent argument is made to the hearts and minds of a few men and women, and where the Word made flesh finds acceptance and "takes," there follows self-generating procreation of faith as natural as beggars sharing precious bread and requires no pushing or coercion.[4]

This is what Paul had in mind, I believe, when he wrote to his young protégé, Timothy. Yes, in our own strength we are weak and timid. In our strength our witness isn't very convincing. But Paul makes it clear to Timothy and to us that as God's witnesses—as His servant leaders—we are to have power through the Holy Spirit.

When Paul was writing to the Corinthian Christians, he told them of the word he received from the Lord during a time of trial: "My grace is sufficient for you, for my power is made perfect in weakness" (2 Cor. 12:9). Like Paul, we are weak, but God's power acts through our weakness and changes us from timid people to become powerful witnesses. As servant leaders, we should use the power that God entrusts to us to lead others to follow us as we follow Christ (see 1 Cor. 11:1).

The Fruit of the Spirit

As the Holy Spirit grants us power for living and leading, He gives us other resources as well. Scripture describes these as gifts of the Spirit and as fruit of the Spirit. The fruit of the Spirit is described in Galatians 5:22-23: "But the fruit of the Spirit is love, joy, peace, patience, kindness, goodness, faithfulness, gentleness and self-control."

I believe that all of this fruit is available to all Christians at all times. As we allow Jesus Christ to be the Lord of our lives, and as we allow the Holy Spirit to indwell and control us, the fruits of the Spirit are manifest in and through our lives. These are not qualities that we can develop or skills that we can learn. The only way to possess them is to be possessed by the Holy Spirit.

This fruit goes hand-in-hand with the power of the Holy Spirit. God does not give us power for the sake of power. He gives us power so that we can live to His glory, and so that we can influence others for His kingdom! It is important for us to understand that our personal weakness becomes an ally in advancing Christ's kingdom.

When Christ comes to live within us in the person of the Holy Spirit, we are empowered to do things beyond our personal ability. He places the treasures of His fruit and power within us. Paul states that the Lord does this for a most practical and functional reason: "We have this treasure in jars of clay to show that this all-surpassing power is from God and not from us" (2 Cor. 4:7).

Building with Love

Let's face it. As servant leaders, we will have different leadership goals, whether we are leading our family members, employees, participants in social organizations, or members of a church. However, all of our goals should focus on two important principles: accomplishing the will of God and building up the lives of all those we lead. God never abuses or violates persons. He wants His servants to grow through all of the experiences that He provides for us. What builds us up builds up His kingdom. And what builds up His kingdom builds us up.

We live in a disposable society. We enjoy the luxury of throwing away paper cups and plastic plates that we use only once. We do the same with plastic spoons and cardboard milk cartons and a thousand other kinds of disposable items that are an integral part of all of our lives. We expect to use up things and then get rid of them. Most of us drive a car for two or three years and then trade it in for another. We expect things to be depreciated with use and to be discarded in a relatively short period of time.

Unfortunately, this mentality frequently finds its way into interpersonal relationships. Some young people use up one boyfriend or girlfriend after another. And many adults hop from one marriage to another after disposing of their former mate. The Church is also affected. Scores of Christians have become known as "church-hoppers." They discard one church for another to satisfy their current tastes or desires.

Those of us who are called to be servant leaders face the same basic temptation—to use people as disposable objects. Our goal in leadership cannot be merely to accomplish our own selfish desires or even simply to perform a task that we may consider important or worthy. We must remember constantly that God has entrusted us with the task of building up people as we lead them to accomplish the will of God in their lives.

In Ephesians 4:2, Paul writes about bearing or supporting one another with love. That is a part of servant leadership. We are called upon to bear or carry one another's burdens, for that fulfills the law of Christ (which is to love one another as Christ loves us). In other words, we should be willing to help others with their problems, encourage them when they are discouraged, and feel hurt when they hurt. Love motivates us to identify with the needs of others.

But the life of love is not only communicated by loving identification, but it also needs to be expressed verbally. In Ephesians 4:15, Paul writes about "speaking the truth in love." Servant leaders need to speak the truth in love. What does "speaking the truth in love" mean? I believe it involves speaking words of encouragement and direction. At the same time, it can involve words of guidance and help when a Christian brother or sister is in trouble or is caught up in some kind of sin.

Paul states that when we speak the truth in love, both the person speaking truth and the person hearing truth will "grow up" into Jesus Christ Himself. What a wonderful and awesome experience! The One who is the source of all truth wants us to communicate truthfully to one another. Servant leaders need to love others so much that they will risk speaking the truth in love even as our Lord speaks truth to us! And as we do, we will grow together in the grace and knowledge of our Lord Jesus Christ.

Such loving and honest communication requires a great deal of risk. I find that those I appreciate most are the people who love me enough to risk telling me the truth. They are my dearest, most trusted friends. This is in stark contrast to what I would call "no risk" or "selfish" leadership. Selfish leadership is destructive. It uses and abuses people like disposable objects. Each time we use people, we remove something from their lives. We consume rather than build; we take from them rather than give to them.

When I was in high school, the word came to us from the Federal government that our entire little South Dakota town had to be moved. A major dam was to be built on the Missouri River, which flowed near us. Some 10 feet of water would cover the beautiful valley where the town was located.

As a result, I spent two summers working on the moving project. One summer, I spent working with a demolition crew. It was our job to destroy buildings that could not be moved. That included a beautiful high school building that was well constructed with brick and block. Much to my amazement, we were able to destroy that magnificent structure in a matter of days.

In contrast, I spent another summer on the construction crew of the new school. I had the task of serving as the "mudboy" for the bricklayers. While it took only a few days to destroy the former building, it took months and months to construct the new. As a young man, I learned a principle that is primary to all of life:

Destruction can be fast and easy; building is time-consuming and difficult.

God has called us to be builders! We have the delightful task of building with a dual role—we are builders of the kingdom of God, and we are builders of the lives of God's people. This is true regardless of the leadership role we may have. As the pastor of a church, a teacher of a Sunday School class, a leader of a scout troop, the parent of children, or a supervisor of employees, I am called to be a builder of lives as a servant leader. I am privileged to carry the burdens of those who follow me and to speak the truth in love so that we may together grow up into Christ. I am a builder for Christ as I build up others in love.

Bob Mitchell, the President of Young Life, expressed this truth very clearly in a moving letter to his constituents when he wrote, "A servant-leader is one whose message is embodied in his (her) life . . . one whose attitude speaks 'acceptance' or willingness to listen . . . one who treats people as individuals and calls them by name. These attributes seem so minor in the total definition of leadership, yet how great a difference they can make in a club kid or an adult questioning Christ's lordship, or to a fellow worker who wonders what it's all about being a Christian."[5]

Most important, it was the kind of leadership Christ intended for us to follow.

Notes

1. The information contained in this appendix was adapted from Paul A. Cedar, *Strength in Servant Leadership* (Waco, TX: Word Books, 1987), pp. 43-57.
2. Russ Reid, "What Ruins Christian Leaders?" *Eternity Magazine*, February 1981.
3. Ibid.
4. Bob Toms, excerpt from an address at ESEC chapel service (used with permission).
5. Robert Mitchell, excerpt from a letter dated August 1982 (used with permission).

PROFILES IN COURAGEOUS LEADERSHIP

As challenges of honesty, enthusiasm, motivation, goal-setting and commitment cascade down on the heads of a new generation of leaders, the natural instinct may be to turn away from the onrush and float downstream with the other drifters. But the urge to serve the greater needs of posterity drives exceptional individuals upstream against all threats to personal comfort and safety. So it is with a leader. Surmounting obstacles demands yet another quality of character—*courage*.[1]

Many past Christian leaders have been distinguished by the courage of their convictions, courage in their public witnessing, courage to proclaim the truth no matter what the cost may have been, courage in their travels. There was Willis Shenk, who lost his life flying to Alaska to evangelize for Youth for Christ. He challenged the largest state in the union with a small aircraft and lost—physically. But the impression made by his sincerity on those who expected to hear from him that evening will live forever.

There was Billy Graham who, at the Forest Home Christian Conference grounds in 1949, questioned whether or not he could preach the Bible completely—a question that drew him into a long night of prayer and wrestling with the Lord. Should he preach what people wanted to hear and expected to hear? Or should he step out in faith and preach what he knew he must? Finally, after long hours of walking and meditating, Graham said in essence to God, "From this point on I will take your Word at face value exactly the way You've given it to me, and I'll never question it again." And he never has. That's why he could say all through his preaching ministry, "the Bible says." This phrase has marked his ministry. It was a courageous step on his part. No matter what the critics would say, he would stick with the Word of God as the authoritative, inerrant will of God.

Courageous Leaders from the Past

If you are a pastor, your challenge is much the same today. People want to hear something that will silence the guilt they feel about neglecting the Word of God. But it takes courage to preach what they need to hear about repentance and righteousness. More and more Christians are interested in New Age "spiritual technology" and "soul physics"—messages that do not require allegiance to the Church or loss of personal power. But it takes courage to teach the message of Christ crucified, Master of our destiny.

Many congregations want personal comfort and instant satisfaction. It takes courage to preach service toward the needs of others, coupled with patience and long-suffering. One way to gain the skills needed today in the home congregation is to look at the skills exemplified in the past from Christian missionaries overseas. Though the places may have been strange and far away, the lessons are near and familiar to the challenge of today's pluralistic society.

Of Cobblers and Martyrs

The period of the modern missionary movement goes back to William Carey, who had the courage to leave his cobbler's bench in Britain late in the eighteenth century and travel to India. His exemplary life and zealous ministry in India seemed to spark the concerned Christian world to new effort in missions. Mission societies began to spring up with the exclusive purpose of getting people to the field and raising the funds to keep them there.

Carey had an unparalleled influence in India. He founded the Baptist Church movement, translated the Scriptures into four major Indian languages, began what is now the largest college and seminary in that nation, and was editor of what became one of the largest newspapers in India.

Missionaries such as David Livingstone, Adoniram Judson, Mary Slessor, Hudson Taylor and others courageously took the gospel to some of the most inhospitable and remote areas in the world. They were, in the fullest sense of the word, pioneers. Many of them were martyrs. They died early deaths as they cut a swath through the wilds and jungles and went to places where the gospel had never been preached.

Miracle at the Mosque

One of the most courageous men of this century was Ugandan Anglican Bishop Festo Kivengere, resident of a country that took the unbridled anger and fury of the half-crazed, self-appointed president-for-life, Idi Amin. For eight long years between 1971 and 1979, blood flowed from the innocent bodies of men, women and children.

Amin was no respecter of persons. A classic example of a paranoiac, he saw the enemy behind every tree, and each threat to him, imagined or real, was disposed of in the most horrible fashion imaginable. Amin's infamous State Research Bureau kept tabs on these "enemies," and through his sophisticated underground network was able to kill, maim and destroy large numbers of Uganda's best and brightest. He used every means possible to perpetuate his power and his crimes.

Yet Kivengere did not allow this to intimidate him or prevent him from preaching the gospel of Christ. Shortly before 1977, Kivengere and a colleague of his were holding meetings in one of the universities in Uganda. Some of the students thought it would be marvelous if these men could share their Christian testimony in a Muslim mosque. The students courageously made the request to the proper authorities and, amazingly, their request was granted.

The leaders of the mosque invited the two men to speak there on their holy day, a Friday. Six hundred of them, upon entering the mosque, took off their shoes and listened for a solid hour to the message concerning Jesus Christ from the two evangelists. During the service, the evangelists detected some shuffling of the curtains alongside the mosque and subsequently learned that about 200 women were eavesdropping to hear the message of Jesus Christ. Some of these women asked permission of the leaders to see if they might enter the mosque to hear these men, something unheard of in that part of the world. Permission was granted, and they entered, fully veiled. For another hour, they, along with the men, listened to the gospel preached by two African Christians.

Shortly after this incident, Kivengere's archbishop, Janani Luwum, was ambushed in a military raid and killed by Amin's troops. Kivengere's flock of faithful, Spirit-filled men, women and children were gunned down, stabbed, butchered or raped. Kivengere was forced to flee the country. Yet, by the mercy of God, Kivengere was ultimately able to forgive Idi Amin. He even wrote a book called *I Love Idi Amin*, in which he wrote, "On the cross, Jesus said, 'Father, forgive them, because they don't know what they are doing.' As evil as Idi Amin was, how can I do less toward him?"[2]

The Christian Church in Afghanistan

Back in 1972, I had the privilege of visiting with my dear friend Dr. J. Christy Wilson in Kabul, Afghanistan. He went there many years earlier to teach English to government leaders in that closed Muslim nation, which at that time was considered the most hardcore Muslim nation in the world. As a result of Dr. Wilson's leadership, a community of believers, from many Western nations, who resided in the capital city was formed. Ambassadors, government officials, teachers and others formed the core of this small Christian group. Dr. Wilson served as pastor.

As a result of the group's witness to the Afghan population, several scores of Afghans began to commit themselves to Christ—despite the fact that if they had been caught, they would either be put to death or, at the very least, expelled from the country. These believers formed a secret society and were known to each other, but they did not dare to publicly identify themselves on threat of death.

Such fear of public pronouncement of faith pervaded through the Taliban-ruled years until the time the American forces took control of Kabul in the war on terrorism. In fact, during the struggle to dislodge the Taliban, two more courageous leaders emerged: Dayna Curry and Heather Mercer, two Christian missionaries who were held in an Afghan jail, accused of telling Muslims about Christ. Before their dramatic rescue by American troops, Dayna and Heather maintained their Christian witness. Although they could have been killed or given life sentences, they sang praise songs while being shuttled from jail to jail, and prayed for their captors.

A Rope of Hope

A veteran Korean Christian told me an inspiring story not long ago about how the gospel first came to his country. Back in the early 1880s, there were, among others, three Korean workmen laboring in northern China. The gospel had recently come to that part of China, and many Chinese had come to knowledge of Christ through the efforts of missionaries. Some of these Chinese Christians, in turn, shared their gospel witness with these three Koreans, who eventually acknowledged Christ as Savior and Lord.

These Koreans were eager to bring the gospel back into their own land of Korea, where there had been no Christians or Christian witness. At the time, it was against the law to bring other religions into Korea, but regardless, these three men obtained copies of the Chinese Bible (which at that time used the same characters as the Korean language) and decided to smuggle a copy of the Bible into their country. They drew straws to see who would have the privilege of being the first to bring a copy of the Bible to their people.

The first man sought to bury a copy of the Scriptures in his belongings. It took him many days' journey by foot to the border, where he was apprehended by the guards. They searched his luggage and found the Bible, and as a result he was killed. After many days, word came back to the two remaining men that their friend had lost his life.

The second man, who had drawn the second longest straw, tore pages from his Bible and buried those separate pages in his knapsack among his belongings. He in turn took the long journey to the border, was searched, and again the Scriptures were found. He was beheaded.

Word filtered back to the third man. He was more determined than ever to bring the gospel into his own land. So, ingeniously, he tore his Bible apart page by page and wrapped each page separately to form a rope. Then he wrapped all his belongings with this homemade rope. When he came to the border, the guards asked him to unwrap his belongings. Unsuspected, he was admitted into his country, and later, very meticulously, he untied the rope, ironed out each page and reassembled the Scriptures. Then he began to preach Christ wherever he went.

Of all the churches in the Third World, none is more exciting, faster growing or more effective than the church in Korea. After the Korean conflict in the early 1950s, there were no church buildings left standing in Seoul. Many of the Christians struggled down from North Korea as refugees and suffered severe persecution. Today, approximately 9.5 million Koreans belong to Protestant churches.[3] Seoul is home to the largest Protestant church in the world—the Yoido Full Gospel Church, pastored by David Yonggi Cho, which now has more than 780,000 members.

How many groups of people and churches in Korea would be "tied together" in the Lord were it not for the courage of that third Bible messenger and his "rope of hope"?

Land of Persecution

Such exploits are not confined to Korea. For many years, Colombia was known as the land of persecution. The struggling Protestant church was under severe persecution.

A number of years ago, I was sharing in a missionary conference at the Maranatha Bible Conference in western Michigan. One day I was having lunch with David Howard, who was then a missionary to Colombia. Dave has since served as director for three great Urbana Student Conferences of the Inter-Varsity Christian Fellowship and is Director of the World Evangelism Fellowship.

Over lunch, Dave sadly related to me the martyrdom of two of his dear young pastor friends who were killed in Colombia, merely because they were leaders in their respective evangelical churches. He knew them very well and was deeply moved by the fact that they gave their lives willingly as martyrs.

But look what their courage helped secure. Today, gospel films are being shown in Colombian theaters, gospel radio broadcasts are being held weekly on the national radio networks, churches are wide open and filled, and it is possible without harassment in most places to freely pass out gospel literature and tracts in the parks of the cities.

Shirtsleeve Saints

It would be easy to dismiss such courageous exploits as the untouchable conquests of a few rare superstars. But that would be a mistake. Today's leaders are made of the same leadership cloth. I simply urge you to seize the torch!

Consider my friend Pete Johnson. Pete is a fellow member at my home church. He is a handyman, plumber, carpenter and builder. On several different occasions, he has gone to Irian Jaya in Indonesia to help the missionary community there with various building programs. By so doing, he has unleashed the missionaries so they can carry on their evangelism and training ministries. Pete has courageously given himself for work they ordinarily would have to do. While he is in no way theologically trained, Pete is using his special skills and gifts in an important and glorious ministry.

Then I think of Denny and Jeanne Grindall from Seattle, Washington. Denny and Jeanne wrestled for some time with the issue of what the Lord wanted them to do in their retirement years. They are warm, committed Christians, and the love of Christ shines through their entire beings; but they both admit, "We are just ordinary people . . . very ordinary."

The Grindalls decided to take a journey, a simple tourist trip, for several months, leaving their successful florist business in Seattle. While they were in Kenya, East Africa, they were taken by missionary friends to the nomadic Masai people. They found these people were living a primitive life; the death rate was extremely high and life expectancy was low. The Grindalls found chickens, pigs and other animals living with humans in the little mud huts. Together, Denny and Jeanne determined they would go back to live among these fascinating people and work together with them in programs of community development.

The Grindalls decided to assist the Masai in learning how to obtain water, build pigpens and develop sanitation facilities. They wanted to share their knowledge in horticulture and give guidance out of their experience. Six months out of every year, this post-middle-aged couple lived among the Masai and were beautifully accepted by these formerly nomadic people.

The once unsanitary huts have been cleaned out, the quality of health has improved greatly and people are living longer. Children are no longer suffering from malnutrition, and the lives of entire communities have been tremendously improved through the loving care and concern of these warm Christians from the Pacific Northwest. With all of this, Denny and Jeanne have borne a tremendous Christian witness, and scores of the Masai have come to Christ.

The Grindalls's example illustrates what any congregation can contribute to the needs of the world or the needs of their community through courage.

Modern Models of Courageous Leadership

Although most of the examples in this appendix come from previous centuries, the models hold true for today. In fact, we do not have to look far to see twenty-first century exemplars of courageous leadership. U.S. President George W. Bush rarely misses an opportunity to express his faith, even though he knows he will take a hit in the polls for it. Texas quarterback Vince Young, after winning the 2006 national college football championship, was quick to thank God, even though he knew reporters would censor his words. Lakita Garth and Rebecca St. James declare before crowds and in the media their commitment to abstinence before marriage, even though they know their call for others to follow suit runs against mainstream trends.

People like Gary Haugen and Lauran Bethel, among others, lead the call to fight sex trafficking of minors and advocate justice for women and children. Nate Bacon lives in one of San Francisco's roughest neighborhoods and reaches out to gang members and low-income immigrants. Diane Moss runs a home in Cambodia for HIV-positive people who are near death. The compassion Diane shows truly is courageous leadership in a place few would dare follow!

We could list Rick and Kay Warren for their fight against pandemic diseases, poverty, illiteracy, leadership voids and spiritual darkness. We could mention Interstate Batteries chairman Norm Miller for his steadfast stance on ethical business practices in a highly competitive industry. We could mention Bethany Hamilton who after losing an arm in a shark attack had the courage to tell Barbara Walters' viewers that Jesus was what really mattered. The list could (and does) go on and on.

What enables you as a Christian leader to make this upstream struggle for Jesus Christ is God's ability to part the waters and reverse the currents. Christ promised a true believer that "whoever believes in me, as the Scripture has said, streams of living water will flow from within him" (John 7:38). As long as you and I maintain the flow of these spiritual currents, we can move against the mightiest of floods. All it takes is courage and the ability to act on that courage.

Notes

1. The information contained in this appendix was adapted from Ted W. Engstrom and Robert C. Larson, *Seizing the Torch* (Ventura, CA: Regal Books, 1988), pp. 113-131.
2. "Festo Kivengere: 1919 to 1988," *The Dictionary of African Christian Biography*. http://www.dacb.org/stories/uganda/kivengere_festo.html (accessed March 2006).
3. "South Korea: Religion," *Wikipedia*, 2003 census data. http://en.wikipedia.org/wiki/South_Korea (accessed March 2006).